Michael Pedersen is a prize-winning Scottish poet and author. His second collection, *Oyster* (2017), was a collaboration with Scott Hutchison (Frightened Rabbit), his third, *The Cat Prince & Other Poems* (2023), is published by Little, Brown. Pedersen has been named a Canongate Future 40, was a finalist for Writer of the Year at the *Herald* Scottish Culture Awards, was awarded the John Mather Trust Rising Star of Literature Award and won a Robert Louis Stevenson Fellowship. Pedersen also co-founded Neu! Reekie!, a prize-winning arts collective known for producing cutting-edge shows across Scotland and the world.

Further praise for *Boy Friends*:

'*Boy Friends* is intimate and confessional. Grief, captured without cliché, leaps from the page. In a story that passes from the dead to the living, from art to life and back again, Pedersen and Hutchison's connection endures.' ***Observer***

'A beautiful exploration of how male friendship deserves more than the beery back-slap of the word "bromance"... An overspill of grief, love and wild romance. Platonic friendships, tectonic emotions.' ***Sunday Times*** (Critics' Favourite Books of 2022)

'The Scottish poet's memoir reflects touchingly on male friendship and masculinity . . . Pedersen pays tender tribute to his late pal.' ***Guardian***

'An inclusive, collective hug; a sharing platter of a book that takes us along for the ride . . . The words take flight and come into land, often with a laugh, on every page.' ***Scotsman***

'Michael Pedersen is a Scottish poet and performer, perhaps the most extravagantly talented to emerge in Britain since John Cooper Clarke . . . Pedersen's language is a juicy fruit pudding studded with Lowlands vernacular . . . *Boy Friends* is an unapologetic paean to the sweetness of a relationship now brutally terminated . . . [and] an entirely endearing addition to the literature of grief and the ameliorating pleasures of memory and comradeship.' *Irish Times*

'Fey and effervescent but shot through with hip, edgy street aesthetics . . . Pedersen simply shows us that the reverse can be true: that men can brim with positive emotion, express their feelings as readily and eloquently as women and be loving and rounded human beings. The change of narrative feels heaven-sent.' *Herald*

'Bonds between male friends have remained weirdly neglected, as if we are scared to examine them too closely. Thank goodness for Michael Pedersen's honesty and humour . . . *Boy Friends* is courageous and generous in equal measure. I am so thankful for it.' *Caught by the River*

'Although Hutchison's suicide looms in the background of Pedersen's retelling, his portrait of their friendship is largely a warm one, overflowing with love and mischief . . . With such candid prose, Pedersen paints an unusually forthcoming account of tenderness between men.' *The Quietus*

'Beautifully, bouncingly and sparklingly written. A book that leaps so assuredly from joy to sorrow, from hilarity to lamentation and back to laughter again, is rare and to be treasured . . . A friend is a masterpiece of nature, Emerson said

– and this book is as perfect a portrait of that natural masterpiece as I have ever read.' **Stephen Fry**

'I was so moved, reading *Boy Friends*, because I found in its pages what I wish for my own son and for his generation of men – vulnerability, deep friendships and a sense of belonging. Michael Pedersen's every sentence sparkles. I loved this book.' **Maggie Smith**

'A love letter to friendship. Michael Pedersen hauntingly captures the exhilaration and the romance of fine friendship and the terror and bewilderment at the loss of it. *Boy Friends* is gut-wrenching and yet gallus too – taking us on a rollercoaster journey of love and loss that makes you say to yourself, more than once, yes, that's it exactly.' **Jackie Kay**

'This sweetly unconventional work by Michael Pedersen, whilst dripping in raw grief, is uncommonly romantic, irreverent and at times laugh-out-loud funny. A delight really.' **Shirley Manson** (Garbage)

'Michael writes with true sensitivity and power. His words burrow down to the core of it all while at the same time offering the soaring perspective of the poet-soul. Deeply felt, carefully crafted, his language firing with pace and wit.' **Kae Tempest**

'There are surely few more toweringly taboo subjects than grief and male friendship, or – dare I even whisper it – love. Michael Pedersen's gurgling, sparkling prose here envelops both in a book that is at once a memorial and a rallying cry to gulp down every joyful, raw, painful, ugly, beautiful breath of life. It changed me for the good.' **Alan Cumming**

'A tender, funny rebuttal to toxic masculinity. It lifted my spirits in the way Ali Smith does.' **Val McDermid**

'As tender as honeysuckle and as bracing as a Hebridean beach. *Boy Friends* makes you feel as if you've gone on a holiday with someone dazzling.' **Mark Cousins**

'A beautiful, moving, life-affirming book about a beautiful, moving, life-affirming friendship.' **Ian Rankin**

'Gorgeous, lyrical, sad and very funny too.' **Juno Dawson**

'Those hungry for the bone-deep truth about grief will devour Michael Pedersen's account of a friend lost . . . *Boy Friends* takes us into the friendships of Pedersen's life; the boys and men who were, still are in some cases, his great loves. *Boy Friends* is a dazzling act of generosity and an entirely original blast of non-fiction.' **Terri White**

'This book is, like friendship, a gift.' **Damian Barr**

'Michael's writing is exactly as playful and invigorating as the man himself. His unique signature of honest vulnerability and bravery is always arresting and generous in a world where most find it safer to dampen and cloak their true spirit.' **Ewen Bremner**

'A lyrical, heartfelt, touching tribute to male friendship.' **David Nicholls**

'*Boy Friends* is a lovely book: bright and heartfelt, funny and refreshing. I greatly enjoyed reading it.' **Andrew O'Hagan**

'Sensitive, urgent, passionate – it reminds us to hold those we love close.' **Cal Flyn**

'Like the best hugs, Pedersen's writing is tight, warm and comforting. Through pain and loss come sweetness and love in a book you'll want to hand to all your friends.' **Monisha Rajesh**

'To locate gratitude in grief is an achievement. To map that journey out with such honesty and humour is a genuine triumph.' **Darren McGarvey**

'A writer that binds us, helps us celebrate the best things about being human and what makes us crackle up with both wonder and laughter.' **Gemma Cairney**

'A kaleidoscopic helter-skelter hedonistic Henry Milleresque hurtle through the grief and shock . . . an elegy for friendship itself in all its lifelong manifestations. Quirkily, deeply, painfully personal.' **Liz Lochhead**

'Honest reflections on the gut punch of grief are a precious commodity . . . *Boy Friends* pays beautiful tribute both to the treasure and joy of friendship and the pain and bewilderment of grief – a gift to anyone who loves anyone.' **Jo Browning Wroe**

'I loved this book. I'm going to tell my friends about it and then I'm going to double my efforts to be a better friend.' **Ricky Ross** (Deacon Blue)

'Part portrait of the artist, part In Memoriam, the rich seam of loss and glory in Pedersen's masterful conjuration with its fizzing lingo, with its wisecracks and insights, makes for a compelling and unforgettable read!' **Daljit Nagra**

'Inventive, true, absorbing, funny, elegiac. This is a wonderful book that voices something very special.' **Helen Mort**

'*Boy Friends* is a funny, poignant and thoughtful exploration into the bonds of male friendship. It's a terrific read.' **Norman Blake** (Teenage Fanclub)

'A book as full of joy and gratitude as it is of grief and regret, *Boy Friends* refuses to consign lost friends to the shadows.' **James Robertson**

'This book broke my heart and made me cry. Thanks, Michael. As if I didn't have enough problems with the end of the world and trying to find ointment for the dog's rash.' **Dominic Hoey**

'Pedersen is intoxicating company – by turns giddy and tender, loquacious and recklessly honest.' **Clare Pollard**

'With staggering sensitivity, lyrical eloquence and razor-sharp wit, Michael Pedersen's *Boy Friends* shines a rainbow of light onto the beautiful and often heartbreaking nature of human connection.' **Emun Elliott**

'This is a gorgeous and courageous book, the writing is so beautiful and evocative.' **Salena Godden**

'This book is a first in so many ways. The world needs more of Michael Pedersen – lots more.' **Bill Drummond**

'Joyful and comic but with a stone of sadness at its centre. A playful and original memoir about the beauty and craziness of friendship; a lament for loss and an assertion of the value and privilege of friendship.' **David Shrigley**

Michael Pedersen

——

Boy Friends

faber

First published in the UK in 2022
by Faber & Faber Limited
Bloomsbury House
74–77 Great Russell Street
London WC1B 3DA
First published in the USA in 2022

This paperback edition published in 2023

Typeset by Faber & Faber Limited
Printed and bound by CPI Group (UK) Ltd, Croydon, CRO 4YY

A CIP record for this book
is available from the British Library

ISBN 978–0–571–36006–2

2 4 6 8 10 9 7 5 3 1

to the friends we love to excess
        yet still
            not nearly
enough

&

      to h-craft   (a-l-w-a-y-s)

Prologue

Ever feel like you were fated to be friends with someone? An alchemy in your meeting, instant fondness – part chemical, part kismet. This is how I've felt about every friend I've fallen in love with – none so much as you.

Now that you're gone, I want to talk about you more than I care to admit. I find ways to meander and u-bend conversations into stories with you at the yolk of them.

While the friendships we forge inhabit us, there's no escaping that one day we'll be without them. They may go kindly with expected effervescence, or, as with you, ungentle and sudden. Either way, grief will come for the heart exposed, like hungry seabirds for a carcass washed ashore.

The invisibility in missing you can be savage. Often it feels such extreme emotion should be worn as a sash or garish lanyard, visually obvious in a manner that commands attention; or, at the very least, avoidance. Think a massive mottled bruise alluding to dramatics or hair going grey from some horrendous fright.

Other times, this couldn't be further from the truth, and the idea that people might bear witness to my grief is humiliating and abhorrent.

I started writing this because I needed a way to keep talking to you, to honour then outlive the loss, and commemorate the impact you've had on me. It's how we stay together now we're torn apart. Like Ernest Hemingway said: 'Write hard and clear about what hurts.'

We often spoke about finding our friends / our friends finding us – what I would chance to call the mathematics of male friendship, yet you were smarter and clearer about; although I can't for the life of me remember how you worded it, because it was more of a feeling than a phrase.

We mused on being older starters, the joy in having all this catching up to do, about preparing ourselves for loving and losing more friends than any other category of human relation – the mettle this takes.

There was still so much I needed to share with you – this, my method of addressing that. This book, which started as a celebration of you and grew into a celebration of many friendships, perhaps all friendship. What began sweet and meek, yet more lurid than I hoped for, was soon striving to be a testimony of survival. Its list of ingredients including heartwood and hidden lilacs – could you call it a paean to beauty? More tersely, it is composed from pain, rationalisation, miles and miles of walking, and long hours staring down the distance.

Funny how missing you has me fishing through my own past, rummaging in the understory of my boy friends. Has me sculpting maxims and conjuring conclusions: if there is a day of reckoning ahead, above all else, I hope to be judged on the friendships I cherished and the love I invested in them.

We're not getting you, my clever bastard, back (not as we know it), and I get that. Accepting the finality of this is a

Herculean task, best buttressed by any means necessary.

How else might we digest its massiveness? A beastly bite of grief where a friend should be is simply unacceptable. I really, REALLY, fucking miss you, and must be getting on.

1

Curfew Tower After Curfew

4 July 2018
Cushendall, Northern Ireland

I am a resident of The Curfew Tower in Cushendall, docked here for the lion's share of this preposterous month.

I have a lime green desk on the second floor of the Tower, hovering above Mill Street with Bridge Street beyond. A picture of you is on the windowsill – the card is porous so light ribbons through it. Its flip side can be seen from the busy high street when passers-by gawk up at this fanciful abode. It is an order of service as opposed to a fan poster. It is standing sentry, setting the pace, watching all. Poetry books by Billy Collins, Sarah Howe, Jackie Kay, Ocean Vuong and Seamus Heaney brood by my side – these I brought. There are two muskets and a gold-painted electric guitar to my right – curios of the Tower, along with dozens of artworks left by residents over the years.

Also with me is a copy of our book, *Oyster*. I wrote the poems, you illustrated the pages, and we launched it with vim and tenacity all over the UK and South Africa. This *Oyster*, jointly parented, was not simply a tangible object but the impetus to develop a show, a ticket to travel and means of securing holidays. More than that, it was and still is a monument to friendship.

Outside is County Antrim: an uncharted hunk of land – its curling coastline, steep gradients and sweeping geometry all new. A perfect stranger, the table-topped Lurigethan Mountain shadows over the town like a protective giant. As expected, it's relentlessly bonny. Its environs boast dramatic coastal walks and a bustling population of oystercatchers. The town is mystical, brimming with lore and a key stopping point for folk music troubadours. In juxtaposition to its phantasmagorical qualities, there's a poorly stocked EuroSpar and glut of neon salons.

These recent months have been more brutal than any I've ever known. Any human hopes to make a statement of this magnitude only once but that's a chimera, though a figment I'll pin my hopes to for now.

We are small and it's unlikely the universe really needs us in the manner we want it to. But the way we look at the world and those that orbit with us, if we're lucky, sparks up a teeny cosmic significance.

I am thirty-three years old when – in the month of May 2018 – I learn we have lost you: a favourite creature and my dearest friend. Your leaving is tragic, abrupt, heartbreaking. Last seen in the vicinity of an iconic Edinburgh bridge, you end your own life. You were thirty-six years old.

You die the same year as Stan Lee, Aretha Franklin, Stephen Hawking and Barry Chuckle – none so young.

There is a condition called hypermnesia where people have complete, abundantly vivid memories of key periods, and can replay the past like favourite films shot in high definition. I do not have this burdensome blessing.

8

My memory of your final months, the close time we spent together before you went, I carry with me to The Curfew Tower (known neatly as Curfew). Here, I chastise, celebrate, mourn, grieve and pontificate this period incessantly. The memories are bloody and fragmented.

Curfew is a most veritable tower, an antique edifice in the heart of the town. Built by one Francis Turnley in the 1820s, you might say it's Cushendall's Eiffel Tower – said to be 'the great object of Mr Turnley's thoughts' it was erected 'as a place of confinement for idlers and rioters'. It is now owned by artist Bill Drummond, who oversees these residencies.

Lurking on the ground floor there is a dungeon – a block of total brick, a dank square in which the entombed air feels heavy and foreboding. The emptiness makes me queasy. I don't ever fully close the chunky oak door for fear the metal lock snaps shut of its own volition. During the day, I pass it in slow motion to instil the impression I'm not afraid. In the evening, I whip past stealthily to avoid finding out whether its haunted reputation is tongue in cheek or more duly earned.

Upon arrival, writers and artists are met by one of Cushendall's best-loved citizens, Zippy. The Guardian of the Keys, he is the sentinel who opens up the Tower and oversees any resident's month-long stay. Zippy is the local butcher and not overly enamoured by vegetarians – although he makes exceptions for those of esteemed character. His shop is called Kearney's Fleshers and is spitting distance from the dungeon's street-facing wall. Zippy jovially checks in on guests and the anointed few receive an invite to his marital home, where he cooks steaks of the calibre guidebook buffs go gummy for.

You were going to come to Curfew, would have met Zippy and known all this. We would have sauntered, ordered from the Specials Board of every restaurant, visited all the watering holes – starting off in Johnny Joe's folk bar and ending up in a seedy pub in Belfast with no clue how we got there. We would have explored the territory and uncovered key locations in propinquity to Curfew where epic scenes from the HBO hit series *Game of Thrones* were filmed. I'd have cajoled you into re-enacting a panoply of the central dramas.

Top of that list would have been a bamboozling occurrence shot in a cave near Cushendun where a Red Priestess (Melisandre) gives birth to a spooky demon (known on the *GOT* wiki as Shadow Baby) that heaves itself out the birthing canal, then launches off to slay a royal chap vying for the throne. It would seem there is a very short labour when giving birth to a Shadow Baby, a smoother and swifter process than most human and animal births and thus ideal for portrayal on a hit TV series; or amateur re-enactments. I would have let you choose whether to play the Priestess or the Shadow Baby, perhaps the swirling birth residue, but not any of the flummoxed onlookers.

An even more important occurrence, which was due to take place in Curfew, would have involved a meticulously curated viewing of Bruce Robinson's 1987 cult classic, *Withnail & I*. This would have been your first viewing of a film I've seen perhaps fifty times and have quoted to you and others, in detail, for several years. I own a copy of the script signed by Richard E. Grant (who plays Withnail – the premier rogue) and vehemently believe there is a *Withnail & I* quote for every situation.

Withnail & I depicts two out-of-work actors, with a penchant for booze, who flee London for a weekend's respite in the country. They do so by tricking a wealthy eccentric uncle into gifting them the keys to his Penrith cottage, where they become embroiled in a dispute with a local poacher, who they are convinced intends to murder them. An unannounced visit from the uncle reveals his prurient intentions and leads to both hilarity and despair. It's callously funny and one of the most exquisite scripts I've ever chomped on.

During this inaugural watching we would have drunk the second bottle of M'hudi, a very special wine, which I had brought back for you from South Africa. You would have become a *W&I* fanatic and demanded to journey to Crow Crag for your birthday later in the year. I would have acquiesced.

Crow Crag (real name Sleddale Hall) is a farmhouse on the north side of the Wet Sleddale Valley (Cumbria) owned by the above-mentioned Uncle Monty, which plays host to a marvellous luncheon and a near buggering. The property has stunning landscape sloshed all round it and lives atop rolling hills; there's a semblance here to Curfew. Amblers from all the surrounding districts get frothy for both buildings' anachronistic brawness. I would not be the first to compare Curfew to Crow Crag, though am unable to do so with you.

5 July 2018

I walk militarily the first few days in order to map the terrain that surrounds my Curfew dwellings. I am its garrison of one human, but not so penned in by the perimeter. Its sheer hills, precipitous paths edging over ocean, and babbling bird life immediately appeal. I'm trying to connect to any circuit, every clockwork, within my reach.

Inside, Curfew feels less temporal, more liminal. I move around it like a tourist drifting through a chic art gallery waiting to be asked to leave; friendless, wondering how to act in the presence of so many hook-hung dreams. Feels like watching myself as part of an interactive exhibition debating whether I survive the work or the work survives me.

Walking has a more obvious purpose. Even when alone, it is possible to walk with friends. Though I carry them in my head rather than linking into their arms.

The impact these humans have had, continue to have, upon me is as life-altering as any devoted romance. A motley crew of friends remain at the top table in the feasting hall of my heart – whether here, gone or elsewhere.

———

Spring 1992 and Edinburgh was suffering, head in hand and soaked to the bones, pelted by another pitiless downpour. A ghastly, slaughterhouse rain, dragged in from the Firth of Forth and gutted over the city. I stood willingly beneath it, ready to be gulped down by my own back garden.

Accidental or not, I had killed my friend Muffin and the fierce finality of that sent flames rollercoastering all over my body. A life extinguished from this planet because of my carelessness and propensity for childish fun.

The hours following the incident outlasted days in their heavy burden. A sadness akin to an island sinking into the sea. I rushed to pad and paper in a desperate attempt to translate guilt, melancholy and loss into a screed of contrition. It felt like a form of inky prayer, this attempt to absolve the sin surging through my marrow.

My note read:

We got a hamster from my / cousin. It always plaed in his wheel. / He made me laahf and he was funny and / cute. But one day I took him out / to give him a wander. He went / behind a box and I pulled the / box out. He ran away. But then he / ran back. / But I did not no so / I pushed the box back in again. / I looked behind me, he was gone. / I shouted for my mum, she came. / We both looked, my sister came. / She found him behind the box / dead. I was so sad. It's like a piece / of my heart gone. I'll never be / the bouy I was befor. My life is rooined. / We got a new one it is nice. But I / still miss Muffin. The new / one plays in its wheel. They / are both lovely hamsters. I love / them both. I love my cats to.

My confession was riddled with grammatical errors, misplaced and mistimed sentiment, acute emotionality, melodramatics and self-loathing. The mercurial flick of a mind failing to connect to the nervous system. A somersaulting reality. A broken machine. Then again, I was seven and this was my maiden voyage with grief.

My mum champions this as my first poem. I see something more confessional, an unburdening.

Some points to address:
- Muffin was female.
- Muffin may have been called Cupcake. She was my cousin Stacey's hamster whom I was looking after whilst she was away on holiday. Neither option shatters expectations of pet names girls are implored towards by society – no coincidence these both double up as common words for a young vulva.
- I have sister called Carrie.
- To clarify the crime at hand: I had crushed Muffin to death. I'd let her out to roam the room, sensing more fun was to be had outside of the cage imposed upon her.
- Once free, Muffin sped off in explorative exuberance (or utter terror). I heard her scuttling between cardboard boxes but lost sight of her. I had removed a heavy box brim-full of toys to check behind. With all clear I subsequently thrust it back against the wall. This slapdash propulsion was the end of poor Muffin.
- Legal Interlude: Elements of Murder:
  ‡ *Actus reus* / the physical act of committing the crime – present.

‡ *Mens rea* / intention to commit the crime – not
present.

‡ *Mens rea* extended – a knowledge, recklessness or
extreme carelessness equating to an intention to commit
the crime – possibly present / jury's out.

The plan was for my message of penitence to be discovered by my parents and in turn relayed to the global populace
(both human and animal). Repentance for a deed I supposed
could never be morally squared. I would then take to the
hills to live in shame. Shame cast asunder the curtains of my
weakling heart.

The irreversibility of these actions made my touch feel
toxic. The form of ascetic banishment I had in mind for such
implacable sin was later visited in Patrick Süskind's novel
Perfume: The Story of a Murderer. The central protagonist,
Jean-Baptiste Grenouille, after learning the art of perfuming,
strangles a young girl, intoxicated by her wondrous scent.
He then takes to the countryside to live in isolation in a cave
inside the Plomb du Cantal. He dwells here for seven years,
living off the land. He's protecting the world from his malevo-
lence, running a daily gauntlet of crisis in his own mind. At
seven, I had not read Patrick Süskind's novel *Perfume*, but this
is the type of inchoate existence I felt necessary to protect the
planet from myself.

In reality, I never made it out the front door. I deliberated the
tear-stained scrawl for such a time I would be found exhausted
and in deep slumber beside it on the living-room floor.

Upon her return, I was aghast to find my cousin Stacey nonplussed at hearing of Muffin's premature demise; she was suitably more interested in recounting the details of her holiday antics. Aghast, yet relieved.

Soon after the loss of dear Muffin I begged into existence my own hamster. I would prove myself worthy as a conscientious care-giver. Not one to shy away from big brand influences, I swiftly named this hamster Pepsi. He was definitely a he. Irrefutably male, his balls would regularly swell to an astounding size, stifling his usual agility and pace. Such body-morphing was not unique to Pepsi: the testicles of male hamsters commonly swell to several times their original size in spring – it's nothing to worry about, the vet decreed, and Pepsi's long, happy life attested to that.

When Pepsi died, I buried him in the back garden in a cylindrical mint green pencil case. A commodious chariot to the afterlife for one of such a size, shape and curvature. I made a wooden cross from foraged branches to mark the spot and dug his grave deep to avoid furtive foxes seeking meat. After digging the hole and laying him to rest I remained in the back garden until all light shrank from sight. For hours I stood there, hovering, like Christ the Redeemer.

From groggy clouds the rain shelled down but did little more than mask my tears, hide tremors and quieten the gasps. The next-door neighbour (Old Elaine) called my mum to notify her I had been out in the back garden in the dark and pouring rain for quite an inordinate amount of time. My mum said that she knew and was keeping an eye on me.

Intransigent and warring against the upset, the wetter I got the deeper my feet rooted into the soil. Eventually, I was fetched in.

I just felt things an awful lot, that's what my mum told me during these periods of emotional turmoil, painting the day's dramatics in positive swirls. I took it to heart, thought of it like a superpower.

———

7 July 2018

Zippy is avidly involved in the local hurling team and eager to induct Curfew residents into the fan fold. I, of course, accept Zippy's invitation to attend a match – out of decorum more than sporting intrigue. And so Zippy picks me up and motors me off, all plumes of patter. It's an away game for Cushendall to Dunloy (whom I'm informed are a shower of pricks). On the drive over he recounts the rules of hurling and some team history before navigating towards his deep fascination with Thom Yorke.

I also learn it is not wise to liken hurling to quidditch. Zippy does not take fondly to such comparison; declaring this to be a sizeable compliment from an inveterate *Harry Potter* fan only worsens matters. Digging a yet deeper hole, I pronounce the comparison a gift to hurling, benefic even. Hurling is the fastest field game on earth, sure, but quidditch is faster on account of the Firebolt broomsticks. Quidditch takes place in the air so

I see no direct competition between the two games despite the stark similarities; in fact it's better framed as a sporting allegiance. Both sets of players, at their acme, move like birds. Both are bruising stick-and-ball games that have been enshrined in literature. Zippy disagrees.

The actual hurling match is furiously quick and appears to me even more physically perilous than quidditch. The ball is battered about – on the ground, in the air, absolutely fucking anywhere. The hurl strikes with scorn. When it connects to the ball with force and precision it launches off hard and fast enough to floor a rhino.

The early evening audience are fanatical and lively but fairly sparse, and so there's relatively little obstruction between them and the pitch – meaning the ball regularly cuts holes in the crowd. Throughout the match the keenest and closest fans have to swerve, duck and (in some cases) leap out the way. Someone's car in the car park behind us takes a thwacking dunt during the game, which draws from the crowd a mix of ribaldry and hushed sympathy.

In any case, Cushendall lose. I try to join in the deflated chatter on the drive back as Zippy issues his crestfallen summary of their sporting paggering. The team, punctured early, started leaking momentum like a burst baw. He reckons they'd accepted their fate by the end of the first half and, to exacerbate matters, the referee was a hateful bastard. I aggrandise my own disappointment not to see the team triumph. In truth, I'm just glad not to have been knocked out. At times, it felt like watching a battle re-enactment.

Counting my blessings, I lope off, less lonely beyond the pale of the crowd.

———

I grew up in Edinburgh: Leith as a nipper, Parson's Green Primary in Willowbrae, then on to Portobello High School in, erm, Portobello. Today finds these north Edinburgh areas – some of the city's most notorious – firmly within the grasp of gentrification. Each has changed drastically since I burst beyond boyhood.

My family were not wealthy but not under the vice of poverty either. All things considered, disparate as we were, my clan was a tight unit with a boisterous breed of kin on either side of the family tree. Just four of us in my immediate family, but with twelve-plus aunties and uncles and over twenty first cousins, our tree had thicker thickets than your common birch.

Primary school was grand enough, though I did piss myself a lot. Pissed myself, out of fear and excitement, a little longer than most other kids but tended to be in the top academic groupings. In fact, before PE and extracurricular trips there would be a general bathroom call out and then a second specific summons for Jackson, Ralph and Michael. Whenever a pool of pish was discovered in the gym hall, we'd be the first assembled for inspection and rarely need the search go any further.

Jackson was the class bully. He orchestrated squabbles, announced fights and certified any romance. He came into his full brutishness as he aged. Ralph, on the other hand, was the quietest in our class, kept to himself, ashen-skinned with a nervous manner. Despite the bonds forged by our overactive bladders, we never mixed in the later life the world had in store for us. Jackson would be in and out of jail, whilst Ralph would find a career in low-level retail.

I enjoyed the *Goosebumps* books series (graduating to *Point Horror*) and would happily dish out a whole pack of Rolos at breaktime to gain favour with friends. That and eating crisps out of puddles as a demonstration of my grit. I would willingly and of my own accord donate the little money I accumulated from guising* to good causes. Sweets, like the ones procured at Christmas, I gifted to friends that came around to play after school.

I was not in the school football team, though enjoyed a successful period in the chess club. I rejoiced in helping my mum in the garden, had my own patch garlanded by pebbles. I would harvest seeds from garden centres to grow (edibles, of course, and a Venus flytrap for its life-taking occultism) and believed rubbing lavender in the palms of my hands would make me run faster – as did my friend Laura. I was right close with Laura, one of the neighbours' daughters, before attending primary. Then quickly became wise to the yucky-girl syndrome practised by my male peers upon entering primary two – as did Laura of the reciprocal silly-boy syndrome.

One of my most vivid memories from primary school is

* This being a common Scottish term for going trick-or-treating around Halloween – disguising oneself in a costume or mask and visiting local houses hoping for rewards of coin or confectionery.

hiding behind the curtain at the school disco (in that same gym hall upon which I urinated), after hearing the girl I liked liked me and might want to dance to a slow song. On top of that, she was considering kissing.

As this was exactly what I wanted, I made sure I hid well away from it. Moored behind a ten-foot curtain, teary about how close to fantastic things I had come. I resurfaced only once the pace of the songs picked up to a 'Cotton Eye Joe' level. 'Cotton Eye Joe' being a fast-fire barn-dance-inspired song by Swedish Eurodance group Rednex. During the song you'd swing various partners around until someone fell over or vomited.

———

8 July 2018

It is two months since you've been gone (could be two days or two lifetimes) and I still spend the vast majority of my time thinking about your voice and the funny and sad things you said. I'm supposed to be writing poems; instead I'm drafting diaries and scribing annals whilst listening to your songs and swooning at pictures.

In Curfew I do try to live offline, in books, on walks, with Word documents. But sometimes I capitulate to the pertinacious summons of social media – where former joys become my own clickbait.

Social media platforms are canny interlocutors, regularly uprooting popular postings from the past to masquerade in front

of us. I did not anticipate grieving would be so intricately inter-
linked with my broadband speed. Part of me thinks I should shut
down my accounts, but too much light dances in through these
digital portals to close them, and tonight the birds are cheeping.

Things that might bring me closer to you:
- attending a common riding while wearing the
  ceremonial pin;
- drinking small-batch cider;
- smoking click button menthol cigarettes;
- spending more time marvelling at far-off planetary light;
- getting a tattoo or two;
- possessing one of your teeth;
- having this tooth implanted into my mouth so as to
  continue to share meals;
- watching quality crime drama.

Then again, this might just make me miss you more.
I must remember:
- the computer screen does not stop staring back.
- the online world's innumerable pedagogues will never
  cease spinning information around their mills.
- myriad digital discoveries will pass me by daily.
- outside in the wet air I'm needed just as much (or as
  little) and only there can my tongue taste the pollen in
  the breeze; can my eyes survey the ocean's foam for the
  arrival of a submarine pipe; can my ears catch the song of
  the grasshopper warbler.

– I feel wisest when walking; walking will loosen the knots in me.

– to find a soft, dry spot before falling on my knees.

– to walk into nowhere and make of it the somewhere it already was.

————

I had plenty of reasons to be terrified of high school – the thuggery of bigger kids, at this stage, wasn't even the front-runner. My fears were woven into notions of having to forcibly mature beyond boyhood – that it would soon be humiliating to still enjoy playing; that my favourite games were on the brink of extinction. I assumed playfulness was set to expire, due to be usurped by bawdy teenage pleasures I knew nothing of. It was true of course, but new games of equal merit would rear their heads and fancying folk would reign supreme.

Portobello High School had many fine attributes: a decent library, a few standout teachers and some exceptional humans. I have friends from there still in my life, friends I don't intend to ever let go of. The school and the denizens that shared it with me are a constant source of inspiration. Its reputation, however, is mixed. Notable alumni are primarily of an arts and sporting pedigree: Gail Porter (model and TV presenter); Ewen Bremner (actor – Spud); Kenny Anderson (boxer); Ken Buchanan (boxer); John 'Robbo' Robertson (footballer); Ali Paton (aka Siren from TV show *Gladiators*); James Carlin ('Drugs Kingpin' from Operation Domino).

Portobello High School at one point had the largest number

of students of any school in Europe. An eight-storey sky-scraper considered to be an eyesore on the landscape. This monolith, marked with fans of charred black on the top floor from the flames of a lift explosion, would later be demolished. It cast a literal shadow on the city.

The legendary crushes on its central stairwell would leave many students bruised. Smaller students were commonly carried several floors past their intended exit point in the torrent of the crowd. That wasn't an excuse, mind you – the teachers simply demanded you wriggle harder next time. Methods of wrestling free from the skittling bodies being a skill fast learned. The risk of being spat at or pissed on from up top, too, was a constant grind. Mostly the piss was administered into and subsequently released from a bottle rather than directly from a penis. I don't think any females ever showered piss down upon me, but I couldn't be sure; mostly the micturating perpetrator was an unknown entity, the echo of their laughter as close as I got to the deviant.

This made Portobello High School one of Scotland's most dangerous buildings in the event of a fire. On top of that, if gale-force winds arrived (not uncommon in coastal Scotland), we'd often be sent home in case the windows blew in. There was precedence for that, so we'd sit hopeful as the winds wailed and the windows began to pulse from the whip of it.

I wouldn't say I suffered from bullying in high school; I got by without anything too painful, but certainly felt an affinity with the bullied – narrowly escaping being a bully's main focus at the expense of some poor soul closer to my own sensibilities. For the first few years, I certainly didn't feel empowered to prevent bullies going about their bullying and that too takes its toll – the craven onlooker. Everyone I knew felt like little pieces of puzzle trying to find a fit before they lost their shape. It's only natural going from schools housing a couple of hundred students into a skyscraper of well over a thousand. With you, I spoke about these trials at length.

In my first week, I did get booted in the face by a third year, Lauren, wearing a particularly sturdy pair of Rockport boots. Rockport or Timberland boots and fluorescent tracksuits (preferably Kappa) were best for blending in at Porty in the late nineties / early noughties. I was walking behind Lauren on the stairwell when a rascal called Junior, flanked in beside me, jabbed her in the arse with a compass he'd nabbed from maths. Junior, cat-like, vanished from sight as Lauren turned around – two steps above and growling down. My lips failed to offer an explanation in the time Lauren allotted, wasting only seconds before slamming her right boot into the bottom of my jaw with a sturdy clunk. I hit the deck. Junior chuckled churlishly. Lauren carried on to class. The rest of the day I turned to stone trying not to cry.

Lauren's friend informed her, 'It wiznae even him. Wiz that Junior cunt.' She shrugged her shoulders and retorted (quite rightly), 'Some cunt hud to pay.'

Pube-less, on one of my weaker days, I remember weeping along with the Counting Crows lyric 'I feel things twice as much as you do' in my bedroom. Sobbing then writing it out multiple times in various ornate scrawls. I'm not even sure those were the correct words. Any which way, that song and others in their oeuvre made me fantasise about life morphing into a *Dawson's Creek*-style drama series. Adam, the puissant singer of Counting Crows, had lit a cosmic candle in my sky. A beacon I'd always known was there, one that I believed would guide me home whenever lost and far away. I did not take quite so easily to Oasis. The Bangles on the other hand, absolutely. I'd recite their lyrics to my first high school girlfriend to win her affections on the Geography Department's glacier trip and later attempt to translate them into French for a love letter.

There were manifold incidents of the Lauren-kick-in-the-face ilk, but in the main part I got through high school by careful social manoeuvres, fickle alliances and sitting in clear view of the teachers. Much of the art of getting by was about timely entrances and exoduses from class and the school grounds. That and where one headed at breaktimes and lunch. All the zones not reigned over by an authority figure capable of placating the hunters amongst us.

Highly out of character, I once chased a kid called Rowley up the road for making advances at my girlfriend. I was elated to have not caught him and recall the chase attempt being appositely lustreless. I'm pretty sure he was *at least* aware of the incident, but who knows, kids broke into sprint for all sorts of reasons back then. The ironic thing was, what I really wanted was for us to be more intimately acquainted.

For the most part, I stuck to the corners and crannies, studied hard and dreamed harder, kept close with my friends.

———

Oyster is off on another reprint and I have to etch a new dedication. Being tasked with this here at Curfew makes it marginally more achievable.

This is a sobering lesson in learning to write about you being gone – something that is not, nor will it ever be, okay. I consider the formidable and colossal void you've left, encasing us like wax, like arms, like ocean. I call upon this same force to unify us, summoning from within it the gnostic pull of an entire galaxy of magnets. The force is you and your draw, a reluctant lodestone and magnet supreme.

I do not want a new edition of the book but my friend back. You do not keep living through these pages – a smoking candle where once there was a gorgeous amber flame. I miss you so much, such heart-aching hullabaloo is simply wrong.

Our book travels on a different axis now; you do not travel with it nor with me – something has to be said about that, I know. I write, I cry, I eat. My grief has an appetite – pretty glad of that.

——

My best friend in high school was called Daniel. I remember we got so close within the group, rumours of us being 'poofs' quickly developed and were virulently spread by wider members of the cabal. I surmise they never actually thought us 'poofs' but would feign a seriousness on the matter as a way of castigating how close we'd become. The activities we enjoyed outside the sanction of the ring (trips in rowboats up the Union Canal, feeding each other's cats, all-night fantasy-gaming sessions) were derided by the ringleader.

Daniel's dad Laurence ended his own life when we were sixteen, in the fifth year of high school. I remember Laurence as a talented man, calm, exhibiting ratiocination with a brain for science and mathematics (sometimes he would tutor us), carving violins for fun. I recall wanting to blanket myself over Daniel's hurt when this happened and admiring his bravery in dealing with death. I thought about how it made me love him more and made sure to tell him.

This was my first experience of suicide, rather deliberate death. It was chilling, sickening and very different to all the forms of death I'd encountered in life or books. Laurence had died quietly in his own home. As a consequence of this, Daniel left our school. His parents weren't together and Daniel lived with his mum and cats – Lucy, Sasha and Boris – seeing his dad at weekends. As a single-parent, low-income household he now qualified for a free place at George Heriot's School.

This was a far more prestigious-looking structure than my school – Renaissance architecture that came with turrets, ambition and the vanguard of facilities; in particular for Daniel, the art rooms. He would utilise these facilities and use a year there to ameliorate a portfolio for art school.

Heriot's was Minas Tirith meets Hogwarts compared to my Porty High, which would have been in the (still cool) arse end of Gotham City. Heriot's was founded in the seventeenth century using money left by George Heriot to care for the 'puir, faitherless bairns', of which Daniel was now one. Then again, likely his move was as much about a fresh start away from weighted gapes, sympathies and teasing.

Despite the school split we remained close. Marking the end of high school, Daniel and I and had a joint eighteenth birthday party in an Edinburgh cellar bar called The Tron – mixing our two cohorts of friends into a heady social soup.

Once at university, we lost touch in a perplexing manner which would trouble me for many years. I think he sort of broke up with me during the uni years – a brusque message about us growing apart post a weekend visit to Cumbria, where I clashed with one of his art school pals. Pride, upset and over-reactions (namely by me) widened the gap to one that would need to be bridged over rather than skipped past. But as graduate schemes kicked in and we both found ourselves in London, we were inclined to meet up. New jobs, a new city and, what felt like, new lives created enough of a distraction to fuzz away the absence during these sporadic get-togethers. Being young, lost and loose in London, wobbling in the titanic tremors of this goliath city, was sufficient justification to call upon the familiar sanctum of an old friend. Why didn't it become more? I guess we were wary of being hurt and dealing with the quickening pace of our graduate roles. That and the fact that both our stints with London were relatively short-lived.

Daniel reached out in 2016 to applaud my appearance on Irvine Welsh's BBC *Artsnight* episode and, then again, when you left. My first best friend offering consoling sentiments on your goneness proffered a port in the storm, just when I needed one the most. It was akin to a knot in a scarf that had begun to choke me coming undone.

My friendship with Daniel felt like my first love in many respects – feeling incomplete without his presence, feeling dumped upon his leaving; pushed away by the person that was supposed to know me best. Losing him was living with love lost and in the odd compassionate message we exchanged was real salvation (bonny as the cackle of a bonfire – the type superimposed on big televisions in posh hotels). I think about him often.

———

10 July 2018

Today is a rummage-around-the-Tower type of day. I will frisk its living vegetation, rifle in its litter, sift through the hay, which in this case is art.

Part of the deal for artists staying in Curfew is to leave a trace of themselves behind. I've time to work out what that means for me but some pottering, poozling and annexing of what other residents elected to contribute (or discard) should help.

In its cloggiest fissures, Curfew resembles a thrift store, except nothing is priced or leaving. Five storeys high, it is teeming with fabulous flotsam.

There are questions I'm compelled to ask of a place as imbued with history as this, whose occupants come then go with no intention of staying. Questions such as: Where are the bodies buried? What secrets still dwell here? What burns in its kiln?

Its skeletons I have already seen; one of them at least.

Today the sky flings spears of light in through the wee windows, dressing every floor. Bright rays corkscrew doggedly into each room, little beaming burglars that smudge the sharp edges of its old furniture. It feels like someone watching. Of course, I'm hoping that it's you.

On the front door frame the height of a hundred people is recorded. It is a Time Lord. Names scribed in marker, pencil and biro; in red, blue, green and black. Leon, Arlo, Niamh, Flint, Tiger, Candice, Parker, Tracy, Westen Charles. Most are passers-by, a single dated entry at the beginning or end of a stay, others grow over the years. I'm fourth from tallest, just above 'Dad'. .

The spice rack in the kitchen is busy, thirty-odd glass cylinders of various fullness. One jar dates back over a decade. The eldest vessels are clustered at the rear with smeared labels. Some of them likely outliving the people who purchased them, who too, perhaps, can now be represented as an equivalent amount of ash.

I find handwritten letters hidden in a shoebox. These are from the past to the future revealing nothing of any great importance.

There is a box of collectable 7-inch vinyl singles with no record player to play them on.

In the bathroom is a toilet and a bath and forty-odd bottles of shower gel and hair wash, each down to a tincture. The mirror wears a steamy condensation of voices. A Kermit the Frog sponge caked in dead skin waits ready to scrub my long boards of flesh. No chance.

By the bathroom sink is a picture of Bill, who's clambered onto the sink and stuffed a good deal of himself inside it. Underneath the picture is a line of text: 'I am wrestling with how much of my body I need to get in this space before I can say I'm actually in it. I go for as much as possible.' It's an impressive bodily contortion, about which I think simultaneously: that sink must be strong; and I wonder if he bruised his shin.

Out the window is a well-concealed garden dissected by a washing line I will later hang my tub-scrubbed laundry on. The fire pit, in the centre of the lawn, is a carpet of powder – a papery wreckage of burnt things, including the charred crumbs of books.

I would not be surprised if there's a stream underneath Curfew, trickling down the hillside, searching for the sea. I put my ear to the floor, breathe in, and listen for its euphonic rhythm.

On the outside of Curfew is scaffold. Even those made of concrete and brick need a little buffering from time to time.

In the natural choice for an underwear drawer, in the top bedroom, there's an illustration of a suited rocker doing the splits with a speech bubble that reads: 'Greetings time travellers of the future. Nice undies!' As my underwear is flamboyantly decorated, I collect the accolade.

Last but not least (in by no means an exhaustive list of Curfew's contents), the skeleton. I will not flag its location and ruin the surprise, but somewhere blotched onto an inner wall of Curfew is a spooky glow-in-the-dark skeleton, which scared the bejesus out of me.

The remnants of the artists that came before spur me on. These lamps of life draw me to conclude that some people passed time here frivolously and left unchanged, whilst others experienced a shudder which titled their axis more permanently. The majority, I surmise, sit somewhere in between.

Today, I feel you most inside, not out, and wonder what you would have left in place of all the music? My thoughts are curtailed, for just like that the rain is on.

Funny how the sun was eye-needlingly bright and now it's drizzle, cloud, the greys.

Funny how the harder the rain falls the more life rises from the earth – a jubilant thought; then again, perhaps it's only to stop us from drowning.

———

During high school I discovered fantasy literature and went through a phase of drawing Tolkien- and Mervyn Peake-inspired landscapes – fairies, goblins, banshees, mountain-top castles, glass-still lagoons with treasure swirling in the belly. A full assemblage of the fantastical, celestial and mystic. This was my way of escaping, on some of the more tumultuous days, into the castles of literary kingdoms. My imagination travelled easily – away with the fairies and who wouldn't want to head in that direction?

Fairly recently, I stumbled upon a folder of fantasy drawings when visiting my childhood home with my girlfriend, Hollie. Highly detailed pieces, fastidiously etched with sharpened nibs and daubs of blunted shadow. Each sketch thought to be a paragon piece was inserted into a laminated pocket.

I divulge my boyhood drawings humbly, knowing you, being a couple of years older, would have been deftly working up a portfolio that would see you straight into art school; a harbinger for a career in illustration.

Nonetheless, to me, this was the type of artist's opus one would hope a lover might happenchance upon. We trotted through the pages, me orating the books they stemmed from and the requiems these stirred in me. It was most satisfying until we stumbled upon a more unusual piece. A quite distressing creation. There it was, shameful as a pishy pants incident in primary PE, a detailed drawing of Rolf Harris. But not just Rolf, Rolf with some egregious alterations.

The drawing I created was Rolf Harris's head deposited on the body of a Chippendale butler. The butler was wearing only tight pants and a black bow tie, the rest just fabulously toned flesh – a muscular torso with gleaming pectorals. The muscles rippled, the silver service dish glistened, and Rolf's coupon blossomed over with a devilish grin.

Quite rightly, I was inquisitively probed about why I had chosen Rolf to etch and why I might combine him with a muscular butler. I had no words or contention. There exists no explanation of this deviation in subject matter, nor linkage into the vinyl cover illustrations that followed in the folder. The style was undeniably mine at this chapter in my life and its central position within the portfolio attested to my sense of accomplishment in the piece. But fuck knows why this anomaly existed.

The problem is, the story has another nipple to it – Hollie knew this, which made the discovery all the more worrying. See, on a high school art trip I had encountered Rolf Harris with elation. We were cutting across a field of sunflowers in France, having fallen behind the group on account of being hungover with reluctant steps. Fifteen, yet the local bar had served us beer and wine without a flicker of suspicion. France is a utopia, we declared. As we trundled up the gentle summit of the field, figures emerged from over yonder. Shadows became chess pieces, then took familiar human shapes – arches and plumpness. Out of the expanding shapes came faces, features, clothes and cheery pinkness. Astonishment. It was Rolf! Rolf fucking Harris. Rolf and his wife and a camera crew.

Turns out old Rolf was shooting a TV series in which he would replicate the works of great artists across the globe. The episode we had chanced upon focused on Van Gogh – whose tragic tale ended not a far fling away in Auvers-sur-Oise. More importantly, some of his more notable canvases were painted in this neck of the woods.

Naturally, we wanted a photo with the Australian goofball and had cameras full of film. He was jocund and obliging, dishing out hugs and deliberating the best angles of sun and shade. We took group and individual shots with Rolf, who beamed the whole way through. Less pleasant, we had to make a swift exodus after one of our group vomited unexpectedly, splashing bile and orange juice over Rolf's painterly shoes. The spew only strengthened the story's currency with our peers. Yeah, I met Rolf. And my pal boaked on him.

This novelty chance encounter with a 'celebrity' was unpacked with vigour on numerous occasions during my high school years. Often concluding with me scampering upstairs to collect my prize photograph. In fact, the picture was nabbed and then gifted back to me in a hand-painted frame by my teenage beau. Like the school itself, this photo has since been destroyed.

The Portobello High School I knew came down in 2016. I miss it marking the landscape and reminding me of the friends I made there and the fear that stalked the corridors. The stairwell crushes have been resolved by the architects of the new building, which looks positively space-age in comparison. The fire-hazard factor of the school has been reduced but Edinburgh has less character for it. Then again, the area itself has changed, with its recent residents proving to be less accepting of the former building's vile charm. Portobello, like Leith, has been frothing up to its cultural zenith in some respects, yet has witnessed house prices and rent rocket as a result. Its trendy new title bringing lots of economic obstacles to those on lower incomes. That said, the muggy ejaculation of gentrification was far from my mind as I readied myself for the university years.

————

12 July 2018

I view the sea suspiciously. The rowdy spill of water I'm looking at is called the Sea of Moyle, the narrowest expanse of wet between Northern Ireland and Scotland. Narrow yet volatile with a propensity for violence. From what I witness, it lives up to its notoriety. It showboats and rollicks, proves itself to be the most vicious of tricksters, most drastic of shape-shifters. One instance it's a big dopey puppy wanting to play; its lapping waves lick across my face. Moments later it's more malevolent than all the fantastical beasts in the novels I hoard – a ship sinker, sailor slayer, island eater; pitiless and mocking.

From this perch, I spy the Mull of Kintyre, Scotland, home. Then learn, from a passer-by, that these environs link into one of Ireland's best-known myths, that of The Children of Lir. Within the tale, King Lir's four children are turned into swans by his jealous new wife / their wicked stepmother – noted to have cold eyes and skill with the druid's wand. The children are to remain swans for nine hundred years until a queen from the north marries a king from the south and they hear a bell tolling. The toughest three hundred of these swan years are to be spent on this slop of the Sea of Moyle. The swanlets do perdure the long stretch but have a right old time of it – assaulted by storms and separated from each other. On the rocky shore below where I stand the children of Lir are rumoured to have returned. I won't finish the tale but will suggest seeking out its ending. It's safe to say, I was absorbed

– being contiguous with where *Game of Thrones* was filmed and out of eyeshot of urban modernity is the optimum state for such fabular immersion.

A stupid bit of me thinks you might have waited for the final season of *Game of Thrones* before leaving us and deliberates the best way to preachify these episodes so as they might reach you – a message in a bottle, an unstamped letter to an unknown address, a narration on a set time and date like a well-produced director's commentary? On this cliff top perhaps the answer lies. So I lean into the wind and shout out to you; voice a blackened wick still smouldering. As I reach the end of the trail, a little hoarse, the clouds shift, revealing a juicy red sun; its strawberry light pouring down, frantic as a nosebleed, onto the sky's pale sheet. The way I see it, a tell-tale sign to shamble back to Curfew.

———

After high school I used my grades to gain entry (for me and my picture of Rolf) to the prestigious University of Durham my dad had advocated for. It was a less than a two-hour train journey south of Edinburgh yet on arrival dealt me a fast-fire lesson on the UK class system. An induction to: school league tables; competitive academia; the 'thickness' of my accent; and the peculiar traits of ancient collegiate universities.

My college was University College – better known as Castle for being housed in Durham Castle. It was the university's founding college, founded explicitly on the Oxbridge model in 1832.

Here there were such things as Formal Dinners, at which a Senior Man would decant a Latin grace to the Master of the College (hovering above us at High Table with the professors and fellows) before we could be seated to dine. These banquets, held twice weekly in the medieval Great Hall of the Castle were compulsory to attend – little Castlemen and Castlewomen would don formal attire complete with gowns for such a privilege.

An even more opulent version of 'Formals' existed in the form of the bi-annual College Feast. All such occasions simply gearing up for the unfathomable extravagance of the hotly anticipated June Ball.

Most students revelled in this baroque gala, yet some did so with a self-assured mockery, as if to assert the ball was try-hard posh, a nouveau riche stowaway on their yacht through life.

It was hands down the swankiest soirée I'd ever been to – there was a string quartet on arrival and royalty in attendance. It featured in *Tatler*'s Bystander column and Mastercard's 'Top Events Money Can't Buy'.

There was a college song called 'Gentleman of Castle', during which us pups were expected to drink a yard of ale out of an ancient yard glass and express fury towards the Senior Representative Committee – 'Nearer still and nearer, on to victory. Floreat Castellum, pride of Varsity . . . Floreat Castellum, balls to SRC!' An oar with shot glasses wedged into it was the alternative provided to the College Ladies.

There were Etonians, Harrovians, Carthusians and Cheltenham Ladies in my year, and such a thing as a 40k-a-year education.

There was a real need for a tuxedo, a scarf collection, moccasins and all manner of tasselled garments. The cricket jumper I had for dressing up in at Halloween became perfectly acceptable to wear to brunch. One chap had a pair of brogues that belonged to a former prime minister.

There was a prince in my year – Prince Guillaume: heir apparent to the throne of Luxembourg – and regular visits from the then prime minister's son.

There was a college porter who could fine you for breaching college laws and a college court in which you could be had up for bringing the college into disrepute.

Durham was antiquated, pretentious and bewilderingly different, full of outré antics and self-proclaimed scallywags – Rockport, Kappa and Timbies were most definitely not best for blending in here. At eighteen, fresh out of Porty High, I fucking loved it.

I was labelled a rough yin rather than softie, a complete turn turtle in the expectation others might have of me (and I might have of myself).

At Durham, I had elected to studied law, the reason being a little wayward. I'd been advised by a mentor (of sorts) not to jump into a literature degree and turn to stone / academia something that was currently such a free-form and joyous pursuit. Keep with language, he said, but don't plug into the motherboard; elect a subject that involves constant linguistic analysis and essay writing but has other elements too. Anyhow, a long night down to a flashback, I decided law was one of the most pedantic interpretations of the English language I was going to come across – cases and people's freedoms oscillated one way and the other based on the interpretation of choice cuts of lexicon. The case name akin to a book title, the case notes the synopsis, and the full legal transcript, the manuscript. In law, philosophical questions constantly arose but had to be fast settled, and that finality, although terrifying, was also awe inspiring.

My most transformational university friendship, the one took me farthest from what I knew, was with a fellow law student called David Sparrow.

Sparrow was sword sharp, politically clued-up, my first London friend. He'd grown up around influential politicians and through their close acquaintanceship had sipped tea and shared gags with world leaders and a pope.

Yet he was a bit of a fugitive in this society – his mum a teacher, dad a safari guide in South Africa – which he navigated with bravura. He was cunning as Steerpike (the anti-hero from Mervyn Peake's *Gormenghast*), just as popular with the capitalists as with the Marxists. From what I witnessed, he could be bootlace straight or zany as a kookaburra, able to unearth common ground or spin yarn with just about anyone. So much so, I never knew who he was hoodwinking – perhaps everyone, perhaps no-one. Either way, I was flattered he clung to me. I clung straight back.

Sparrow smelled like old books – not in a foosty way; it was a rich and nutty smell, sweetened by rain. He also looked like Frodo Baggins (aka Elijah Wood). Consequently, it was in the queue of a bookstore that we crossed paths. Later that week at breakfast, in the Great Hall of Durham Castle, he would cease eating his fry-up and declare baked beans to be fine for a mouthful or two but then they just get tedious – don't you think? I agreed, though I didn't, and discarded the rest into the slop bucket, leaving the table hungrier than I should have been.

He inducted me into his world, both in terms of the Durham elites and, on trips to London, the pace and timbre of a well-connected big-city life. Via his shepherding, I ended up in manifold unexpected settings; one night took us from a private soirée at No. 10 Downing Street to drinks at the East India Club within a matter of hours. Being hosted by a prime minister weirdly met my expectations. Entering the domain of the East India Club, however, was an altogether more disconcerting experience. Yet Sparrow's sangfroid seeped into me and so I bounded jovially into each bizarre situation.

I was clueless as to what the East India Company represented and would have likely not entered if I had been better informed, but Sparrow made the experience feel cavalier, more like gatecrashing a stuffy party, us the victors for having illicitly gained entry. On arrival, I was equipped with a visitor's tie and blazer and found it all very amusing when an elder statesman started enquiring about my schooling. All of us doing a little role-play, I was as happy to chat to the puffed-up oddballs as they were to me. The quietest man in the room was undoubtedly the most interesting and poured us all large brandies from his special bottle – at that point, a drink I'd never tasted. The old sport strained his jaw and raised his bushy eyebrows when I shot it back like cheap sambuca, then seemed to lighten to the grotesque act and poured me another. I left with his gold-embossed business card and kept hold of it for years after, as if one day it might buy me safe passage into Parliament.

David Sparrow was like a turbid art-house movie I never got to the bottom of, yet something about him kick-started the motor in me. Mostly kind but sometimes cruel, he thumbed me like a trashy magazine, I read him like a clever comic. We lost touch, started seeing other people and our social groups became incompatible. But when all is said and done, he pushed me forwards, challenged me into challenging myself, and credit where credit's due, showed me *Withnail & I* for the very first time.

Keeping watch over myself and Sparrow was one of the tutors at our college. He'd interviewed us both, vetted us and placed us in the same little colony under his surveillance. He encouraged, empowered and tested our friendship, equipping us for the inevitable separation that lay ahead.

This same tutor helped me out financially with occasional administrative work, allowing me to plough through a rickle of paper applications for the law school, my bias roaming free. He put me on a crash course in coffee drinking and wine tasting, recognising at once I had no acumen in either and might need to pass myself off as someone with a palate in the near future. Teaching me how to swindle the snobs, he willed me to succeed – it was above and beyond scholarly investment. Say what you will about the concept of mentorship within collegiate universities, being one of his initiates served me well. He sought out the wonky ones. We remain friends still.

I arrived in Durham (Land of the Prince Bishops) hyper-emotional and sentimental, remained so, but something chaotic stirred me, something unruly. It had always been there, like the hiss of a radio in the background, but with the chance university brought to fashion myself anew it boomed much louder. I answered its hurricane call.

————

14 July 2018

I start to recognise Cushendall's faces – shop attendants, dog walkers, river watchers, shuffling teens on corners, perfervid rain runners, ice-cream-regardless-of-the-weather fetchers of a mettlesome making. A whole community of new people I never had an inkling of months ago, and with their existence my global cognisance grows.

Some of these faces give me the unavoidable nod of acknowledgement, where it's easier to let on than not. Others muster a willing smile, which leaves me wearing mine and catching the next person I pass off guard. Reader, there's a winker in my midst, the gift that keeps giving. Certainly, I wink back. Then there's a few folks who stop to trade in the affairs of the day, test-run a new joke or make a soap opera of the weather. These are those that might welcome me in if I locked myself out.

I'm connecting the dots of Cushendall like I once connected the dots of Cambodia, like I connect dots in Caledonia when greeting faces still finding their feet. Despite this grand procession of newness, the world still feels ineffably smaller; the loss of you has knocked the big cosmic balance off kilter. Favourite friends are, after all, the rarest species.

In revisiting the life cycles of seminal friendships, I am yenning for warm humans whilst equally yearning to relive, so as to rejig, a part of my own past. With you, it's not like that. Sure, we had the odd tepid moment or petty squabble, but nothing I feel the need to rectify. Nope, with you I was content with our story, I simply want more. Yes, I celebrate every crackling-crusted, crouton-topped moment of it, but, jesus fuck, we were only getting started.

————

My most intense friendship following Daniel and Sparrow was Rowley. My friendship with Rowley permeated my early twenties over a three-to-four-year period. We'd been at the same high school but never clicked.

Rowley's face was always lively, a spiky form of handsome, fully furnished in expression whilst not appearing animated – it was classic, like an old ballroom with high ceilings that had fallen into disrepair. He could be devastatingly charming when he chose to be, intoxicatingly fun.

Rowley and I reconnected at the tail end of my time in Durham, during the exam leave period when I was back in Mother Edinburgh. It was a 5 a.m. encounter, both of us still up and sloshing about house parties on opposite sides of the same road in Portobello. Rather, Rowley was spotted in a swaying languor in the street outside, as our group squeezed the final flecks of revelry out the night. Rowley spied this social chowder and stomped into the garden, peering through the front window like he was watching the finale of a Nordic thriller. We beckoned him in and I was immediately spellbound by his ululating chaos and harsh caw.

His giggle gushed glitter through the room; it was completely out of control. He thrashed his eyes over us one by one, riffing off everyone's modified appearance, mocking his own with total indignation. He looked like a romantic poet, like Syd Barrett, and served us buffoonery alongside profound sentiment. The front of his right trainer shoe was hanging off, fixed back in place with rainbow gaffer tape. I instantly loved him and didn't want his absence to become a thing; he was all: eat the world, or it eats you.

Our Edinburgh-forged friendship didn't take full flight until immediately after I left Durham and moved to Nottingham. Nottingham was the next stop on my academic relay race. I was there for a year completing a postgraduate course, during which Rowley visited frequently and even moved into my small bedroom in a shared flat for a few months. I came back to Edinburgh for another year after Nottingham, procrastinating before I was drafted for service in corporate London. We spent so much time together over this period we began to interblend, alive in each other's skin. Of many memories, I'm not sure if they're mine to stake ownership in or his.

Our friendship was a substance-addled romp through petty crime, addiction and indulgence, but ultimately an obdurate love affair. We were poor, had thrown our phones into the ocean, slept in parks and on beaches, brandished a faux homelessness and were recklessly entwined.

During the Edinburgh chapter of our story, we would conceive elaborate plans to fund our desired peripatetic lifestyle: a computer cafe heist, extorting donations from unwilling patrons and a salmon-poaching expedition. We did not follow through with all of these; others we did. I'll spare myself the sentence and leave that there. Suffice to say, my lifestyle choices would not live up to scrutiny if I was to run for public office.

We also did not follow through with our band The Capricious. We had one rehearsal in a house the council rented for a single mum called Sophie, who mostly kept the kid elsewhere in order to occasionally roof Rowley. Our rehearsal was calamitous. There was no amplification or orchestration, yet despite all these failings we remained certain of redefining the musical zeitgeist. I barked out poems as Rowley and another dear friend (Owen) thrashed around on a bass guitar and a steel-string. Rowley searching for his lead vocal in my landsliding wordpile, instantly rejigging the stanzas into improvised verse and wolf howl.

To fertilise these little song sprouts, several bottles of Frosty Jack's super-strength cider were taken, which go surprisingly well with turkey drummers and oven chips. I fear, alas, rather than galvanise any growth, we drowned each song seed in the pit of our bellies before the root could break beyond its shell.

Later that week, Rowley smashed my steel-string against a wall and put his arm in a fire claiming to be invincible. He challenge-dared that one of us would yoink him out the flames before he flinched. And right enough I tackled him back from the blaze after ten seconds of the amber tongues lapping around his extended arm. I wonder still how long he'd have let the fire toast then scorch his flesh, but I'm resolutely glad we didn't find out. I have never doubted his gallantry.

We nary mentioned the band again outside of our own inner monologues and the odd chat-up attempt – vaunting our unhatched virtuosity for a free drink or an invitation to an after-party.

Rowley and I would love each other publicly, kiss frequently, share beds, tears and dreams. Over this period I snogged many of my male friends in states of ecstasy and appreciation. I kissed Rowley the most.

Ours was an unhealthy dependence on each other and we suffered from a unique pariah complex – we were on the outer ring of several friendships, trying so hard to remain so. Any time life eased up or our complex dilemmas began to resolve themselves, we would stir the pot so as to cast ourselves back out to the edges. Hurting people who cared for us to test the extremities of their tolerance, whilst rhapsodising their loyalty afterwards (to the level of nuisance).

We saw ourselves as key culprits in a gruelling yet necessary battle against mediocrity, ennui and inertia. We were undoubtedly lost ourselves. This was very much an alone-together compact, burning any bridges that couldn't hold the pair of us at our most volcanic. Extolling our friendship above all others. To me, to us, this was a whittling down to the most vital form of loving. A seemingly unlimited mutual forgiveness driving our ability to dedicate passionately and abundantly to our friendship.

I was loyal to him to a level which alienated me from other friendships and narrowed my social circles. My ex-girlfriend from high school, for example, didn't speak to me for many years over a misunderstanding in which Rowley pinched some money, booze and tobacco from her flat when we were invited round for lunch. The thieving was intentional but also spontaneous, rather than premeditated, and not part of the grammar of the day from the outset. It happened in my absence and ignorance. As she showed me some of her framed photographs up on the mezzanine level of her apartment, Rowley began to loot. When I patted him down, he returned everything he had purloined, with a brisk yet cheery apology as if he couldn't see what all the fuss was about. The situation festered for some time, and I still get the odd shifty glance from Porty High alumnae who moved in her circle.

But, to me, he was worth it – the judgement, the ruckus and frays, all written off. He was ruthlessly devoted, my most trusted accomplice – anything I would have asked of Rowley he would have done for me. When I was not in his company, he was constantly championing my poetry and person (mostly in that order) with an *amour fou* that fortifies me even now. He once called up Daniel after I detailed our estrangement and

49

lambasted him for his deplorable oversight. Far from being embarrassed about this, I felt my honour had been restored and a wrongdoing put right. There was something unconquerable in our dastardliness, something of great value in the amount it cost us to stay together. Nobody else would feel so vulnerable without me and a lack of Rowley made life too miserable to bear.

Rowley was lashing out and punctured by tragedy, his mother having died young after a vicious run with alcoholism. I never got to the bottom of whether she died of physical illness or whether it was suicide. The trauma coated his actions in a salve of forgiveness and made him all the more loveable.

I once brought him to my family's Christmas gathering (on my mum's side, less radge) – about twenty of us, BYOB and a buffet of discordant foods and flavours that would have been laughed clean out of the auditions for an M&S advert. Despite the humble set-up, Rowley bounded about the party fully riveted, declaring it his favourite Christmas in living memory. He thanked everyone profusely for the invitation and doled out more hugs and kisses than stolid men might grant in a lifetime. My grandad, a plumber, gifted him a piece of copper piping – cut, filed and polished – for racing up and down the fretboard of a guitar. Full of appreciation, he welled up then rang like a bell. For Rowley, the alternative to this Christmas had been a pot noodle and soaps on a tiny telly – he deserved better.

I always found friends who wanted to love too much, who collided rather than simply met – it fitted what my heart was looking for. This came from a dissatisfaction: that the emotional intensity coursing through the characters in books was barely evident in the most day-to-day acquaintanceship. I wanted to squeeze every note out the day and kept my antennae on for the crackle and flare of broken life forms. I soon found like-minded sorts, literature-worthy.

I've written several poems about Rowley and once mapped out an outrageous novel entitled *My Upas Tree*. *Upas* is the Javanese word for poison and, it seemed to me in my early twenties, a very clever name for a book about a tragic friendship. The novel waded in the myth of a tree that boasted a nonpareil beauty alongside the ability to produce a juicy poison; the toxins seeping into the soil and fending off its enemies. I'd later discover the title had been used to repletion by the likes of Alexander Pushkin and other literary savants.

Heavy-heartedly, I ran from Rowley down to London – it was becoming too dangerous for my health, for the future writer I wanted to be, for keeping hold of anyone that cared about me. We were supposed to go together. Me engaging in a legal training contract in a huge avaricious corporate firm and him intending to doss about in my fiscal foliage. It wouldn't have worked for long and I'm lucky to have escaped the compact – a rare moment of restraint amongst the milieux of mischief.

Rowley's fidelity was coeval with his pride, and so when I didn't take him to London our communication simply ceased. He had a phone only intermittently – the number perpetually changing – and didn't use any social media, so it was easy for him to disappear off my radar. We stopped communicating in 2009 and I've not seen him since.

Haphazard as it was, my friendship with Rowley remains a testament to how fast and hard you can fall for friends and the unflinching loyalty they can offer. I showed Rowley all my shades of being and he helped me ink things over. I mostly yen for Rowley in a way that doesn't require satisfaction; it's enough to know how much we loved, how we bandaged up some wounds together. Although I've not had eyes on him, I do have his postal address (not salubrious quarters) and have sent him every book I've written. I will continue to do so. He was (and is still) to me a wonderful, mis-wired weirdo of impetuous passions.

From what I garner, his life since I loved him has been hard and full of hurdles; in softer moments I will the world to shove us back together.

———

15 July 2018

Bafflingly, a friend, Janette, is holidaying in County Antrim and arranges to come for an evening visit. Janette and her daughters had been staring up at Curfew just hours before, looking for signs of light, listening for songs. I'm not sure where I was hiding, inside myself perhaps; or, more likely, inside one of our stories. Either way, I'm grateful to have her here now.

Apart from Zippy popping by to check in and keep me abreast of the week's hurling fixtures, no-one has yet entered this domain. And even he never strays past the entranceway. No-one, not even you, until now. Janette moves around Curfew as if she's always been here, bringing sparkle to even its darkest corners. She greets the space with such warmth it causes me to take better ownership of it. We drink villainous wine, talk about books and sex, and then drift towards Johnny Joe's.

If local geography begins with a pub, Johnny Joe's would be base camp. It is a former coaching inn, a big dwelling house that's morphed into a bar, complete with roaring fires and a salmagundi of ornaments. The rooms have the quirky architecture of space being used for a purpose for which it wasn't intended. Its inhabitants are a mix of stoic barflies and tourist visitants, with enough chatty regulars keen to present themselves as local patriots to bridge the gap. On a busy night it is instrument-filled and alive with stories and song. On a quiet night I can stake my claim to a private nook and sequester myself.

I ask for a half-pint of something and Janette returns instead with a pint a piece and shots of sambuca and tequila. This shot selection is a favourite loosener of my friend The Cous and so I guzzle them back with dynamism as if saluting an old friend. It's a warm sticky night and we talk so bright the stars creep closer to eavesdrop on our juicy bits.

Leaving me in a plume of smiles, cheer and clanking jewellery, Janette departs promptly in order to make her home-time curfew, so as to be back for the kids' lights out. I return to my

Curfew, teeth caked in boozy sugar, and sit in the dark of the dungeon for as long as I can.

———

Just prior to my divorce from Rowley and moving to London, I spent two months in Manchester. There I made a friend called Jake.

Jake carried nicely pointed features and a sinewy frame; drainpipe denims looked boss on him, mod shirts too, his shoulders shapely as a coat hanger. He was tersely labelled a soppy git by some of his hardier friends. Jake, however, had a tongue that flicked flame, an electric edge and energy surging through him, so didn't get much gyp from those all hot and bothered by his lovely emotions hatching.

In the infancy of our friendship Jake and I, along with two other friends, collectively lived in a flat at Parkers Apartments in north-central Manchester. This was a run-down hotel awaiting renovation and the next surge of gentrification to justify a facelift and a new shiny exterior. I was a short-term resident, Jake was in and out; the two friends had taken the lease longer term. It was a lax arrangement: four of us whisking ourselves into cream in a single-bedroom slot that became a prized home to rival its history as a fast pad for one-night stands.

Jake liked to climb cranes and danced with the stiffened aplomb of a chiselled Manc. This dance astounded me: harsh, jolting movements that remained captivatingly rhythmical – the body loosened yet taut as if being held up by wires inside the flesh and controlled by a joystick from above. Galvanic, both perfectly stable and completely erratic, true to life with Jake.

He seemed particularly heedful of my stories, especially any that resembled parables or involved a moral, and was catalysed by any conversation that led us into fact-finding. I lapped up his sermons vying for betterment, envied his ability to make a friend of anyone within a few choice words. In his company, I felt safe with life's quickening pace.

Jake and I quickly let each other know that we were smitten for this alliance, that we had connected magnetically and that this felt like the start of a friendship that would heave and clutch us together. We had started a painting together that would move from thin lines by wee brushes to viscous handfuls of paint smeared across canvas, chests bare.

What Jake did one night would arouse a shift in me. He halted the disorder of the after-hours drinking party and built a circle with the seats. The five of us in that loop had spent the night together in impassioned confabs and tomfoolery – oily, sweaty, many smiles unzipped as we pounced around town, sneaking into clubs and private parties, wagering our faith in future glories. Jake wanted to honour the night; the hot spring of emotional juices flowing through him, he wanted us more deeply together. He explained that he'd love it if we could each go round the circle and profess one great thing about every human in it. Something special, a gift just for them. We all committed with varying degrees of emotional depth, given the freshness of some relationships compared to the mature oak of others. But we did commit and each of us remembered this ritual like we'd engaged in a séance.

Jake would sometimes interrupt conversations to let the group know a recent good deed one of us had done that he was either recipient of or witness to. He took time to credit friends and express his admiration. He would often do this softly and subtly and other times boldly and brashly with braggart brio. It could embarrass people or take them out of their comfort zone, but it mostly sweetly pleased. I was agog a couple of times at folk's humbled reactions. Especially in what would be considered rowdier social settings in tired old boozers, where the company was caught between runs to the bookies or drug deals in plain sight.

At first a little in awe of his methods, I was but a casual observer. I soon found myself a devoted convert. I began by feeding back to Jake the love-filled approbation he was dishing out so freely to others. Then took to spreading the seed further, with and without Jake in tow.

Jake taught me to pay homage to my friends regardless of the company and was a source of vitality and righteousness within the realms of friendship.

Every time I finish an excellent book, I announce a list of reasons why it was memorable. I wouldn't want it thinking that I thought it an arsehole or, worse, that I was incurious about it. This method of celebrating the greatness around me I apply to all my friendships. This is something Jake instilled in me: acknowledge important chapters, the beginnings and the endings. For Jake's genius, I'm forever grateful.

It was also Jake who first offered and advocated heroin to me, taught me the ropes – how to smoke it and how much to use.

Heroin crept slowly into my life in a very social way but never became all-consuming. First it was something that would happen occasionally after parties in Manchester and London. Something that was smoked on tin foil through silver pipes, or sprinkled into roll-ups. It evolved into needles with relative ease and was nearly always administered by and with Jake.

I'm a tad reticent giving this period its spotlight, as I was still working full time, kept myself upright and financially stable. It's not the *Trainspotting* story, that's for sure. Although some of the folk I came into contact with were living that, I was not. All the same, it wasn't without some deadliness.

I caused a few throbbing pains in delicate organs, vomited a little more than I should have for one so young and lithe, and had a bad attendance record at work. Jake once put air into my lungs to pull the peach and pink back into me after my breathing slowed and blue and green started seeping over the flatline of my cheeks. Whether this was a veritable overdose or not, I'm unsure. I wholeheartedly believe Jake stopped me from having a more definite answer to that question.

There was a very short period of time where my heroin usage was becoming more regular, whilst still based around Jake's presence. When I found myself injecting without Jake, I realised my pupillage was complete and it was likely time to take umbrage. That's to say, delete any numbers I had for accessing brown and keep away from Soho slingers. Jake going missing in action – locked down by family and friends for his own safety – and his visitations becoming less frequent, certainly oiled the wheels of this transition.

Jake's quarantine was because he was getting lost in the wind; he overcommitted and had several overdoses. One involving some time in a coma and severe social estrangement. He would later be labelled Junky Jake and ostracised from a familiar friendship group – by their and his own volition.

About the most ashamed I've ever been is coming up to visit Jake, fresh from the clutches of his coma. Ashamed not because of his disposition, but because of our wholesome Sunday lunch descending into a heroin-smoking session in a public park. A park by Manchester University rife with picnicking students. I was his afternoon custodian and, though persuasive, those that loved him thought better of my duty of care. This episode made for a particularly bitter encounter on account of having to purchase the product off an acquaintance of his that had just lost his son in a devastating fishing accident. Jake's acquaintance being dependent on our score to fund his own relapse worsened matters further still. Dependent on me overpaying and tipping him for his trouble in coming to us to deliver – a much mooted element of low-level drug transactions.

I left Manchester for London on the train four hours later than anticipated, tasting of cheap orange cheese from the sandwiches I had vomited up. Plagued by flashes of the acquaintance's globular nose, peppered in blackheads the size of pinheads, sinking into his grief.

———

16 July 2018

The next day Janette returns with her kids for a tour of Curfew.

As these sort of lookout towers have become outdated compared to the skyscrapers and radio masts that commonly populate horizons, it's enthralling to see the youth so enchanted by Curfew. As soon as they're inside, they're wrapped up in the mystery of it and instantly more receptive to legend and folklore. The same goes with me and the books and movies I consume here – they're Curfew-enhanced. Just like my ability to pay vigil to your memory, these watchful old bricks bolster every element of my cognitive deep-dive.

Curfew enables me to write about reality as if a form of fiction; helps foment, and muddy, the life-and-page separation. I suggest to the kids that it's the age gap between Curfew and me that keeps me on my best behaviour – Curfew flaunting its life-guru status over my tyro ranking. We must all respect our elders, I tell them, whilst only half believing it – them respecting their mum; me respecting Curfew; Curfew respecting the Lurigethan Mountain; the Lurigethan Mountain respecting the Irish Sea; and so on.

What I don't tell them is that, really, it's the looming presence of Curfew's dungeon that keeps me on my best behaviour. Drawing the noise out of its stilling, stifling air is all part of the janitorial shift.

What I also don't tell them is that when I get jittery edging past Curfew's dungeon, I think of you. I think if something spooky comes out of there and meddles with me then I've confirmation of the supernatural. In the confirmation of the supernatural is the probability of an afterlife. And in the probability of an afterlife is the possibility of parallel universes – domains more utopian, abstruse and vast than this one. With that in mind, some spooky cunt appearing from a dungeon to meddle with a visiting poet suddenly becomes something pretty phenomenal.

Despite all this, I still carry a glass bottle for protection, knowing fine well I cannae glass a ghost. What I can do is be brave enough to endure it and reach back; open the door, let the ghosts in.

Janette and her pups truck off suitably amused and it feels only right to see myself out alongside them. I take the steep hill to the left, up Ballybrack Road, rather than follow the natural pull of cliff and coast.

———

It was London in 2007, and there was me and Ted and Rodriguez in my flat on Hibernia Street. Ted, too, bided at this address whilst completing a PhD at UCL in chemistry. He had gained a first-class Master's degree from Durham – where we'd met – and would later complete post-doctoral research at Harvard. But his time in the Big Smoke collided with mine and so we bunked in together – the stint, for him, comparable to flying a blimp through a meteor storm.

The Rodriguez I refer to here is not Sixto Rodriguez – the singer thought dead from the 2012 Oscar-winning documentary film *Searching for Sugar Man*. Although I have reason to believe that until the film came out and foiled his charade, this Rodriguez may well have been posing as him. Unlike Sixto, he had not been working in Detroit factories spreading political liberalism nor was he of Mexican descent. He was in fact a Brazilian crack cocaine and heroin dealer mostly found in the Soho area of London during the ghosting hours. Akin to Sixto, he had the music in him.

Rodriguez had fled Brazil, undercover and with calumny close at hand; from Brasília to London on a passport he claimed to have acquired from a leather maker. The fairest dealer in Soho, Rodriguez would get a good price in a timely fashion. A gentleman amongst the rowdy hordes who'd stung me and my cadre on numerous occasions.

He had committed a Série A crime in Brazil and packed a tragic backstory to match it – one with which you'd sympathise yet caveat. You'd say, 'That's the sort of crime I wouldn't be ashamed of committing for someone I loved.' You'd say, 'Good on him' to your buddies but 'That man went too far' to a lover. You might consider, at night in bed, whether you too would carry out these criminal actions but would find it hard to reach a conclusion. Me too. It's safe to say, Rodriguez's actions surpassed the type of self-administered justice a reasonable citizen would employ.

Essentially Rodriguez was a man on the run who'd stopped running for a while, a penniless rover scratching his way through life. Now here he was with us in north London.

On Hibernia Street was a cocktail bar that was rumoured to launder money and only opened its doors once or twice a week, serving extravagant potions at a loss. The pawn in the operation was a goofy, unskilled barkeep named Joel who let us concoct our own drinks behind the bar for little or no cost. Outside of Joel's glitzy hub, this strip of Hibernia Street was dank woodland colours, moss in grass, old match-lit stoves, screaming kettles and cheap tissue. Most popular were stale Irish pubs and fried chicken emporiums with the same name cobbled together an assortment of ways – Best Golden Fried Chicken and Finest Fried Golden Chicken being close enough to shadow box. As well as sizzling poultry, booze and drugs were available cheap and around the clock. Those with sinister intent and a little silver want for nothing around there.

After a full-throttle Sunday evening of consumption with Rodriguez on the streets of Soho, I suggested he come back to our abode for a sleepover. I hadn't ruled out a trial tenancy period but was yet to raise the matter with flatmate Ted.

Alas the rock I'd bought to spend the night with had dissipated into our lungs quicker than expected (as these things do) and a 4 a.m. taxi run to the car pack of a notorious Lambeth housing estate proved necessary. Quite a lengthy journey across London, when the moon held a little blood in it, but needs must.

Upon arrival, we kindly requested the cab hover around the corner, informing the driver this business would only take a minute. 'Wait here,' Rodriguez said to me butter soft before alighting the vehicle. He had eyes as clever as we want stars to be, that could in a nanosecond morph into sharks fixed on prey. Eyes that had stared down all weather with ears finely tuned to recognise the coming of the rain. I knew he'd breezed through dangerous situations that would send my bones bundling back into their limbs and shuck the plucky out of me. Even in his laugh there was the sense of someone searching for something lost / anticipating the battle of getting it back.

I heard a commotion out the cab window as two wiry bodies sprinted across the car park. Exiting the vehicle and snaking around the corner, I saw Rodriguez pressed up against the wall, palms pushing at his cranium, cuffs slapped around his wrist with vehemence.

Having encroached upon the scene, I, too, was questioned. Denying everything other than us meeting a friend to parley, the law spat me back into night, shepherded off with a stern talking to.

Turns out, Rodriguez had managed to swallow the product before the plain-clothes officers rudely interrupted. The dealer had escaped over a hedge – perhaps part of the police plot or just blotted in bad luck. Either way, poor Rodriguez was kept a while longer.

I got back to the flat at 6 a.m. still buzzing, deciding in retrospect that it was for the best our activities reached a surcease when they did. After all, tomorrow was now today – Sunday, firmly Monday – and my second week on the job as a trainee solicitor at a top London law firm.

———

18 July 2018

Zippy and his wife Steph invite me to a barbecue run by Kearney's Fleshers at Cushendall Sailing & Boating Club. It's a postcard-pretty night, the air still, sun glowing, shadows of art deco triangles. All the key ingredients for alfresco feasting – so it's bound to be busy, boozy and bustling. Thing is, I'm feeling fragile as cracked glass from all the elegiac poetry skulking around my mind, and so the natural impulse is to shirk out of it. The trouble is, it's not so fun shirking out of things without you – the rewards are less alluring, the rationale is more bleak – so I goad myself into going.

Besides, the sailing club, unsurprisingly, flanks a stunning slash of sea and serves as the starting blocks for one of my favourite walking routes – a saunter that takes me past Red Bay Castle and Glenariff Beach, where I always take off my shoes and socks.

I meet Steph en route and by the time we arrive Zippy has already disappeared behind a miasma of smoke. Using a spatula to clear the view – fanning and thrashing as if swatting flies – he gestures us to grab a plateful. We do, plus pints, and sit on the sun-hot wall and scran. Steph is well kent here and so as we're finishing up a squad shimmy over. She inducts me into the group – family and friends and local familiars. I latch onto the scruffiest of the bunch, who's curious about Curfew living and a keen walker. The rest of the night passes quickly, all jabber and jollity, glasses clinking, and babies passed around friends. Zippy doles out a hundred-plus burgers from behind his volcano-smoking grill, joining us for a final slurp.

I leave on a high, surer of my verdure than when I arrived. Funny to leave good company and think, 'Got away with that.' Got away with what, Michael – being human? I suppose so.

I can play the extrovert – haptic, cool and self-assured – far more comfortably than acknowledging I'm having a down day. A day caught in the bog of missing you. It's a trickier conversation than merely mimicking my sprier self. Just because yesterday made sense and the talk came fast and smoking doesn't mean today will. It's as much of a risk as turning the page on a book or flicking the channel on the TV.

In this case, the rub worked out. Although sometimes socialising when heartbroken might feel like crawling over hot coals, the memories that carry us through these moments are instruments of love.

———

London got easier for me. I found my spark between the rail and the track: changed fast enough to outrun my enemies, kept straight enough to get where I needed. Like an oyster changing sex then changing back – the chameleon of the oceanic kingdom. I kept the faith of the legal boffins I was employed by, enjoyed London's burgeoning live arts scene and had a wild enough time on the social fandango to ensure the more rambunctious parts of me were sated.

Not only that, I also met a quasi-mentor in a Scottish artist (though very much an international citizen) called Bréon, who offered fuel beyond the corporate world's insipid stew.

Bréon, although a couple decades older than me, was youthful and nymph-like, with a current fluxing through him. And soon I started publishing poems in magazines and journals. A healthy dose of knockbacks kept me from getting anywhere near cocky.

I finished the two-year training contract I was bound to and was able to leave the fancy firm obligation-free – even with some spirited handshakes and amiable references. Jesus, I left a qualified solicitor in the Supreme Court of England & Wales.

Walking away from a highly paid, extremely sought-after position as a solicitor in London merited a mixed batch of reactions. It was termed 'brave' by fellow trainees – most of whom are now Partners with behemothic incomes, mortgages and real-estate investments; some of whom will retire millionaires in their forties. A high school pal, Danny, simply texted 'YAS' and sent a YouTube clip of a Tennent's Lager advert in which a downtrodden Scot escapes the London rat race, hot-footing it back to the Celtic motherland, where he is immediately uplifted. The song 'Caledonia (I'm Coming Home)' soundtracks the scene.

On the other hand, the decision was labelled fucking moronic by members of my family who'd financially supported and cheered me on through law school.

I had decided to leave the profession and travel to Cambodia. My dad was the toughest opponent of this decision. He'd grown up poorer than I can fathom. Da and his brood of six siblings were born into a single room in Edinburgh's notorious Arthur Street slum with a faither fierce as pots boiling over – baleful beyond the bark of this book. When the slum estate came down in the late fifties, their family landed a 'near-parkland' council house in Lady Nairne after initially being allocated space in the (more notorious still) Niddrie area.

In the pictures of my da as a kid he's wearing ill-fitting hand-me-down clothes. He also had humiliating after-school jobs, like picking up animal shite from Holyrood Park (back when livestock wandered freely over those grassy plains) to sell around the houses. In adult life, he worked his arse off and stoked the fires of me thinking academically; he wanted for me prosperity. To him, jacking in a coveted position in a world-leading law firm was not too far off being the personification of worry. Doing so to head to Cambodia to write poetry – as I had opted for – was what he might term a kamikaze career plan.

But fuck it, I might have become a greedy cunt, plutocratic, crooked.

My mum and dad met in The Sheep Heid pub in Edinburgh's Duddingston Village in 1974. Mum was seventeen, underage, Dad just eighteen. They were engaged six weeks after. Dad had lost his eye just a few months earlier in a nasty attack with an air rifle; the compensation allowed them a deposit on a flat near Leith. Before they spawned us bairns they travelled Kenya, cycled around Orkney and acquired three cats – Merry, Christmas and Fatty Lumpkin.

Mum, too, had been grafting hard since sixteen – Woolworths; into social work; nursing in old folks' homes, the maternity ward, sick kids and then twenty-odd years as a nursery nurse in Leith. More of the hippie mentality, she loves poetry and was not so irascible when it came to my abnormal life choices.

Nowadays, my mum frequents Edinburgh's umpteen independent bookshops requesting my books. She's not there to purchase my humble tomes but to ensure they're given prominence within the shops' displays. I've scorned her for this and though she assures me she's not telling them she's my mum, I'm dubious.

There are no writers or artists in my sprawling family, no doctors, lawyers, dentists, accountants, journalists, or other 'top-tier' professionals. There's a varied bunch of skillsets though: mechanics, plumbers, hairdressers, cleaners, binmen, tilers etc. – so plenty of intelligent banter and stooshies, rowdy celebrations and prolific breeding. At the annual getthigethers, now hosted in Cousland Village Hall on account of the growing numbers, there can be up to five generations in the same room (my grandma is a great-great-grandma). I get right into these shindigs and am there whenever I can make them.

I do note that my grandma (wee Jessie Lee) cleaned the house of a known writer couple. Stealing a swatch at their chic apartment and dazzling bookshelves when picking her up, I definitely romanticised the literary profession. Wee Jessie made her mark and had bestowed upon her: a dedication in the book of one of the writers (Sue Innes); and a character named after her by the other (Jo Clifford).

Anyhow, Cambodia was only a year away in the end; the parents simmered down and even came out to visit. It was a period of wide-open spaces, tracing steps into a messy past, of percolating joy and sadness, and learning to better read the ripples. I picked up a modest amount of the Khmer language, mastered a few recipes, taught English at a local school and rediscovered a love of riding bicycles.

I thought about the mistakes I'd made in London and enjoyed being far away from them. I sweated through a great many things: spiritual, sanguine, surreal and sinister. My mind churning over which facets hinder and boost us in the making of friends – our prickles, pollen and petals. Things pertaining to childhood that thwart our ability to relate to people in adulthood. One such fissure of thought I turned to was that of fears and pleasures, or, in a more evolved form, phobias and fetishes. Spare me a moment for memories that travel fast.

Through adolescence, I employed many measures to avoid stickers in day-to-day life; making every effort to purchase fruit and veg unlabelled. When popping coins into charity pots, to dodge the attendant nailing me with a sticker, I would approach their pot whilst they were busy chatting with another coin dropper, and then skirt off with ninja stealth. By the time the coin clatter alerted them to my presence I was an apparition.

Fear of stickers is known as pittakionophobia, a rare but serious fear of stickers and sticky labels. Aye, it's not up top of the phobia league table alongside the likes of spiders, heights, and clowns but extreme cases of pittakionophobia have been logged. Like most phobias, it is essentially a strand of an anxiety disorder.

Apples: the thinner and more piffling the stickers, the more I wince – stickered apples are amongst the most serious offenders. Unlike with the kiwi, you're expected to eat the fetid stain the sticker excretes upon the apple. I tend to take them off with a knife and drop them in the centre of the bin so they twirl to the depths rather than sticking on a rib halfway down – hovering like demons ready to climb back out. The fruit still needs to be washed viciously afterwards. You have to be ready to eat it too, for any heavy-handed dissection almost certainly pierces the flesh, beginning the browning.

I once listened to a *New Yorker* fiction podcast in which a character was described as so lazy he ate the sticker of a green apple rather than peel it off. The image is known to have infiltrated my dreams.

Bread: those fucking yellow wispy curls of death noosed around the top of bread that people fasten on and off myriad times until the sticky jizz of it has near evaporated, carpeted in filth. I hate them most (a *bête noire*).

I didn't always feel this way about stickers and can't surgically pinpoint where or when the revulsion first erupted. I was fine collecting football stickers in primary school. I recall being attracted to the thrill of uncovering rare glistening finds (otherwise known as shinies) and the precision of placing them upon their predestined slot in the album. About the football data, I was less concerned. I was more enrapt by the bustle of the trading floor at breaktimes than learning what teams the players were shackled to or whether they had any prodigious skill.

My sticker nervosity comes after this, born from, I think, empathy and pity. As kids got older and sticker collecting became uncool and mockable, sticker albums got pushed to the sidelines. This is not something I got mawkish over; I was happy to move on. The games that developed got more adult in sensibility, but in essence seemed to simply be about chasing things. The stickers on sweets, fruits and other foods, however, remained an ever-prevalent threat.

I'm not sure if there was a particular incident, yet at some point kids developed the habit of sticking stickers onto other kids. Often splatted straight onto faces or haircuts; insolently onto rucksacks; or cunningly planted on the back of jumpers and jackets to avoid detection. As is the way when you're the butt of a joke, there's laughter from your peers. Upon discovery, some would snatch the stickers off in chagrined fury, others would sportingly join in with the gag – remove the sticker with a blithe chuckle and proceed to pass it on.

Grievous incidents could go unnoticed a whole school day before the sticker fell off of its own accord. A pernicious few would not be spotted until the sticker-bearer got home – the victim removing it none the wiser as to when it was affixed or who the villain was.

To me, this was the seedling to the bullying impulse taking sprout, the earliest incarnation of bullying I can elucidate. I remember always finding it really difficult when kids teased each other – often becoming more unsettled than the victim – especially friends trying not to lose face in front of a stronger-willed or more dominant presence. It would break my heart when buddies would end up brawling by accident, showing themselves to be the plaything of a mischievous schoolyard overlord.

If there was an antithesis to the sticker complex growing up, be it a fetish or not, it would be polyester silk. I loved to stroke those soft woven silky satin fabrics. The smooth allure sucked me in young and enslaved me ever after. The standout and most troubling example from my youth involved my sister and ballet – or more specifically, access to a silk leotard.

When my sister donned this leotard for lessons, I would chase her around the house like a baby terminator tasked by the creator. The task at hand: tackling her to the ground and rubbing my cheek against the soft patch of silk stretched over the belly area for as long as I could pin us in position.

As might well be imagined, my sister was not overly enamoured by this transaction. In fact, she was not sold on the idea of a little brother, let alone one dead set on facially caressing her belly during the anticipatory moments before a ballet lesson.

I was born on her second birthday and immediately renounced – 'I don't want a brother for my birthday,' she yelped. 'Please send him back.' Minus the 'please' – that's just to soften the blow. The bites, nips, pinches and bruises she furtively inflicted upon me in the years after attested to her aversion.

She was sly and dastardly; I was doting and gullible, pining for sibling approval. Once biting into my mum's new coffee table on my sister's command only to be instantly grassed on and subsequently scolded. Blubbing too hard, and conflicted by the truth, to be able to offer any defence.

Another such desperate move to inject myself into the games of my sister and her pal, saw me pissing in the garden and showing off my willy in all stages of relief. More lamentable, was letting them cut off my curls with *my* first pair of crocodile scissors in a game of hairdressers. My mum was horrified and heartbroken. I've grown them back now and am holding on for as long as they'll have my head as a canvas. A sibling friendship was not one that arrived in my life until post the high school years.

My mum, in order to lure me away from my sister in her ballet tutu, opted to purchase sections of silk ribbon from the local sewing and embroidery shop. I would stroke and suck (when touch wasn't enough) these portions of ribbon with such vigour they would near disintegrate – requiring seasonal replacement.

Even now, when I'm due to be in formal social situations, I avoid wearing items of clothing I know boast a superior silk label beneath their folds. The pull is too strong, it draws me out the present moment and suddenly my hand is busy underneath my top. Concealed fingers undulating can arouse suspicion of a more salacious sort.

During my law school exam period I had to resort to more drastic measures and cut out all silk labels from my clothing. One minute I was studying *Carlill v Carbolic Smoke Bomb Company*, the next, a glance at the clock revealed, an hour had passed with me transfixed on the silken slopes of a captive label. Time loss like this during study periods is one thing, hours off the clock in exams another thing altogether.

There's no universal scale to this corporeal romance, no Scoville chart of sensory fire. A fingertip-to-silken-material peculiarity factor evokes an irreverent disregard for notions of quality. Mostly, it's the more synthetic the better. I was flabbergasted to discover pure silk's crunch compared to the sweet lullaby of a polyester impostor. Like towels, most silken labels have one side soft, one side rough. On the occasion you get a double softy, it's best to clock off for a while.

The charisma of synthetic silk is perhaps culpable for my falling short of the first class and into the 2:1 category. That and an unplanned trip to Stockholm during exam leave with a Portuguese rocker by the name of Lobo (Riic Wolf). He did pay for the excursion and teach me the pleasures of melting blue cheese into cooking sauces though, so we're absolutely square. In fact, he reckons I owe him a holiday.

Chewing over fetishes and phobias kept my thoughts busy in Cambodia. But more significant than stickers or silk was the time I spent thinking about friends. The friends I missed the most, the ones that truly mattered.

What became apparent was that many of my most seminal friendships are in some way lost to me – Daniel, Rowley, Jake. They did not fade or waltz gently into the rafters for a breather. We did not reach the natural phase of life where we realised our paths must part. Each friendship was a love affair, yet one cut short and fractured – a vessel lost to a squall with a hull full of fish.

I do not know how I did not see it before – truly I did not but *Withnail & I* is a story of best friends clinging together as the world manoeuvres to prise them apart. For their own good they must split, but it doesn't make the move any less maddening. Two cuts of the same cloth completely separate but for a few straggling threads, filaments that should fall away if yanked apart, not near destroy themselves gripping on for dear everything. Haunted by Shakespeare as threats puncture the plot, the story of *W&I* is one of friendship at all costs.

I had never spent so much time on my own as this year in Cambodia. I didn't have a phone or a postal address and had only occasional internet. It was the apex of my life experience with isolation and alienation. By the end of the stint, I had uncurled a calm within myself but then the urge to squeeze bodies and smooch faces became insuperable. After a year away, it was friends that called me home.

———

19 July 2018

I down tool from writing a poem about you because my first post arrives c/o Kearney's Fleshers. The delivery consists of two items: the first is Katharine Kilalea's novel *OK, Mr Field*; the second is a sterling silver cross. The cross is modelled on a drawing of yours and has become a talisman for many. A talented fan hand-crafts, and charitably distributes, them in paean and so thousands of these crosses have begun appearing around people's necks in recognition of the love there is for you. The cross is double-barred, repurposed religious imagery, indicative of your explorative nature and forensic wit. I slip it on and pick up the book.

Katharine Kilalea is a much cleverer poet than I am. Her debut novel comes nearly ten years after the arrival of her debut poetry collection, which was nominated for prestigious prizes.

After hearing Katharine Kilalea read for the first time, I lolloped home to Kentish Town, smoked a generous serving of crack cocaine and sent a rambling message to her on Facebook full of nebulous accusations of privilege. This was 2008, I was twenty-two and out of sorts. I hadn't met you yet.

The correspondence ponged, orotund and wrapped in chemical delusion. I suspect I was envious of Katharine Kilalea and attracted to her words, wisdom and aplomb. At points when scripting the message, I forgot to whom I was writing or why.

Within this diatribe, I made an absurd statement claiming to be the living manifestation of Ted Hughes's 'bullet'.* I had not read enough Hughes to make such an audacious claim, despite feeling like I had.

I had hoped within my lexical lunacy Katharine Kilalea would identify an amiable genius she would feel obliged to nurture.

---

* I might stress, claiming to be Hughes's 'bullet' carries little to no gravitas or pertinence. It's likely I was invoking the manner in which Hughes's words connect to the body when deftly executed – with the precision and power of a bullet fired from a gun. But then again, who knows, it's a finicky business trying to wire into the version of myself that authored this tripe. Nor would it be time well spent.

Instead, I had made an egregious claim to Katharine Kilalea, which did not, as intended, exhibit my constellation of precocious talent. Rather, it oozed then popped, as is the way with things written by immature, ragamuffin-admiring trainee solicitors. I'm not sure I even came across as Scottish, which is customarily unavoidable.

What I should have said was that I really loved her poetry – not least because it reminded me how far I had to go.

Katharine Kilalea, without response, deleted me as a Facebook acquaintance and came off Facebook entirely. This was many years before it was cool to do so or Mark Zuckerberg was a public figure worthy of rebelling against (despite some of the likeable aspects of him portrayed by Jesse Eisenberg in hit film *The Social Network*). Katharine Kilalea was, as to be expected, ahead of the curve.

In Curfew, I swirl my coffee and it slops out the cup onto my book, phone and the puffy rug – moistening the crumbs of crackers wedged between fluff. Somewhere far off, yet under the same bucking light, I imagine Katharine Kilalea has also swirled her coffee. It does not spill but leaves the cup of its own accord, halos the room and whistles into her narrowly open mouth, barely touching the tongue so as to pleasantly caffeinate without a whiff of coffee breath.

In Curfew, a lazy spider sits under the plant rather than make a web, waiting indolently for the falling cadavers of flies. I imagine Katharine Kilalea's spiders have turned vegan, eating only botanical debris; her plants unlike my plants are not dying and will not see any spiders starve.

When I told you the story of the time I messaged Katharine Kilalea asserting my imperious notions you laughed and wanted to see the message (thankfully long lost), concluding you were glad I wasn't taking those drugs any more. We were both a little proud and agreed I could be an idiot.

Despite the fact that she is South African, I surmise Katharine Kilalea would not have been as much fun for you to drink cocktails with at Johannesburg Airport until we missed our plane to Cape Town. I don't doubt, however, Katharine Kilalea *is* fun.

In trying to write this poem for you, I, of course, think what would Katharine Kilalea do? Yet, as far as I'm aware, Katharine Kilalea did not know you (at least you did not mention this) and has not a bunker of abundant memories to reflect upon for content. Memories that have triggered tears in Scotland, England, Wales, Northern Ireland, Republic of Ireland, Australia, New Zealand, Spain, Malawi, France and Dubai (an airport change but I'm counting it). I understand that crying is not a component of literary lustre, but when mixed with my own poetic experience I hope Katharine Kilalea would agree that, on this occasion, I'm better suited to the job of writing this poem about you.

I resolve that you're both too big for a best-friend poem and never too big for a best-friend poem.

Of course, the Katharine Kilalea I speak of is only part Katharine Kilalea and part a fictional Katharine Kilalea I know to be me and, to a lesser extent, you. I have a deep love for these manifestations of my mutant Katharine Kilalea. Ever in love with you.

Katharine Kilalea is an impeccable writer and the novel, thus far, is excellent.

———

We met because I booked you to play music at an event I was curating. In a sense our first meeting was strictly business, but then that's apocryphal. Your performance came within Neu! Reekie!'s fledgling run – we were a maverick venture, paying crumbs of what would have been your usual fee. You were an established artist with an international output, known to sell out shows and cause overcrowding when appearing at Scotland's indie venues. You played for us because we'd piqued your interest, because you adored poetry, because you'd been in our audience and liked the sensitivity in what we produced. You played because you were a champion of art budding and the grassroots.

I emailed over the invitation, you said thanks and that'd you be chuffed to appear and that you didn't think you were cool enough to be part of our scene, so would naturally accept. You were cooler than us all but humble as fuck, which made you even tastier on the tongue, a leafier and greener good.

Sometimes a stranger's stare lands so purposefully it's safe to assume they've seen part of the future yet to unfurl. This is the way you first looked at me.

It was a sticky June evening in 2012, I met you on Edinburgh's Royal Mile, guitar in hand, and led you down Trunk's Close into the Scottish Book Trust. Led you into their starkly lit presentation hall, which hosted all our nascent shows. Our set-up was beyond basic and our audience intimate, but our collective verve was unquashable.

We served bottled beer cooled in ice buckets for an optional donation, the room darkened was lit fuchsia and hot pink, my mum took the money by the door. You said you were going to keep it clean tonight but then dismissed this notion – that marshmallow-melting gooey grin of yours heating up the room. See, Liz Lochhead had just showered the audience in savvy smut and punchy profanities, and so the floodgates opened. As you began singing, you stepped away from the microphone and padded gently around the room, crooning up towards the balcony, coating every inch of the place in your mellifluous tender. Listening to you that night felt like levitating above the skyline catching clouds together. I never fully drifted down.

I learnt you lent yourself to being lit and people liked to light you. You looked dashing under even the most unforgiving spotlights and harsh fluorescent tubes, but especially in a Caravaggio style contrasting light and dark. You were *chiaroscuro* canvas-worthy.

Some people look best sketched in charcoal, smudged and smeared, others in graphite pencil with the hyper-detail of a sharp nib – you flourished in both, a palette of pastel and autumn colours. Your face felt complete: total in its arcs and contours, soft edges. You were consummately bearded, furry, hair wavy, walnut with auburn flashes and the odd ringlet.

But it was your brown eyes that hooked us, those smoky lanterns. I've never seen such depth in a gaze – all the bits of you kept hidden in the bottom drawer would gush out these peepers, known to swallow people whole. Your eyelids, when closed, held us in a thrall of softness, as theatre curtains holding back the show. All that spark and sentiment cooped and ready to pour out.

After the event we swapped numbers and concurred that we'd have to meet and talk about matters both silly and supreme. Discovering we lived fifteen seconds from each other was surely reason enough; who were we to scoff at such ethereal reckoning?

Our friendship blossomed as many others do, by witty text message and frequent trips to pubs, concerts and eateries. In our texts I would see emojis alongside the words before the quotidian use of emojis bled into communications. In the friendship came the arrival of something I never knew I needed; something I could have waited an aeon for – something I couldn't put my finger on then and still can't quite articulate now. It was like a combination of déjà vu, finding an old love letter, and being gifted a hand-knitted cardigan from a friend no-one knew could knit. It grew like vines – leafed, flowered, fruited.

Dwellings so close to one another was part of the flora of it – linked by postcode, by local store, by last-minute flippancy; hunted by the same postie, hectored by the same gobby magpies. I would chat to you smoking outside pubs when I passed with the shopping. Then I became the person in the pub waiting with the drinks for your return. Finally, I would just start going out onto the street / into the smoking pit, so as your puffing time didn't stymie the chatter. Every second cigarette perhaps – after all, you have to let a person look up at the moon, point their eyes and predict the coming season.

We remained interested in each other's writing, shows, protean thinking – yours bigger and bolder but mine all appealing in their unfettered optimism. I learnt many things about you, things I sometimes expressed in poetic sentiments – on which you'd request, like an editor, further clarity:

'Your walking pace is that of the day waking late in summer, chirruping daft denials as you peel down the street,' I'd say.

'Your laugh like a cavalier kite gliding above a loch on a clear yet unpredictable morning,' I'd say.

'We look like new mountains that appear overnight tricking everyone into thinking the sky had always been marked this way,' I'd say.

'Put it in a poem,' you'd say.

Over the next few years, our friendship developed, aged and evolved, in what were intense bursts. I came to realise there was not a single social situation that wouldn't be improved by you being in it. Like cheese on pasta; a little capsicum in the mix; sprinkles or a flake; an extra scoop so it's just the right amount.

There were years of feasting and toasting and getting up to speed with where we'd been before. There was plotting and jesting and hugging into the stories that were harder to hear. There were shows and trips and lots of times that separated us, then brought us together again – you moved to America, then back, I moved deeper into Leith. You performed at my first book launch in 2013, you illustrated my second book in 2017 – it became also your book. I always walked taller when by your side, and not because I was taller (although I was) but because I was so proud to be close to you. I think this was a common one for many of us who were lucky enough to strut beside you.

The timeline of our friendship was a punchy June 2012 until May 2018, an express train, astounding in the ground it covered. Understanding the darkness behind your spirited candour, the beautiful rawness in you, was its toughest ask.

It is easy to compare you to a bear – it's not the animal I'd choose, which I've yet to pin down; I just know that a bear is too easy to be right. Maybe a Malaysian tapir, a favourite of mine upon first visiting Edinburgh Zoo. These dappled charmers are primarily solitary and cover large territories communicating by high-pitched squeaks and whistles, super distinct. They're characterised as crepuscular but enjoy light and a daytime nap in the sun. What a bewildering belter of a beast – 'mon the tapir.

I called you many names, my most sentient creature. You were a wizard of human emotion, casting spells of song against the menacing forces that rallied against us in kingdoms both above and below. You were consistently processing the great cliffs of human experience that would tumble down upon us – sculpting from the rock majestic shapes. Your imagination was vivid and abundant; fantastic reality enough for me. It came across starkly in your illustrations – the morose made funny, dolefulness shadowed in love, every petal of wonder.

What truly made this friendship sing was telling you all the wonderful things you made me feel and hearing them bounce back. I was in love with how I felt around you. I still am.

———

20 July 2018

Hollie comes to visit. One day we take a trip to the Giant's Causeway and mingle with Zippy and Steph; the other I share something of the best of bits from my multiple walks. Throughout her stay, we turn Curfew's top floor into a den, dragging the second single mattress up from the lower-level bedroom and joining both mattresses together on the ground, bed frame free.

Hollie and I watch *Withnail & I* with chalices of wine. The wine is M'hudi Pinotage. To strengthen the ceremony, we have a wee nibble of hash-infused chocolate left by a previous resident. The *Withnail* watching is swiftly followed by a viewing of *Ring of Bright Water* (adapted from Gavin Maxwell's much lionised novel). Not the most romantic filmic double billing, I'm informed, but there you have it. M'hudi is sipped throughout – clutching a cup of it, clenching and curling my tongue in delight, I announce how truly remarkable it is to be drinking M'hudi in Curfew.

As you know, this isn't just any old grog. M'hudi is the most important wine that my lips have ever met. Though it links many friends together, it starts with you.

———

You and I tried M'hudi Pinotage at Shepherd's Tree Lodge in South Africa in October 2017. The place was a sanctum. We had snuck off on safari, a sojourn wedged in between shows in Johannesburg and Cape Town on the South Africa run of our book tour. We had shared many bottles of wine over the past few years of our intense friendship but none so bewitching as this.

M'hudi had a historic and inspirational story we knew fuck all about. What we did know was that it made us giddy. We became astronauts sailing in its plummy ether, eyes wrung around stars.

M'hudi was uncorked on our first night at the Lodge, shortly after we returned from an eventful safari run around Pilanesberg National Park. Pilanesberg is bigger than Glasgow's Kelvingrove Park and Edinburgh's Holyrood Park combined – the word 'park' does its imperiality a disservice. It is in fact some 550 km^2, set in an extinct crater. We were celebrating a day of tremendous wildlife spots and being on an actual animal safari in Africa (as seen on TV).

I do not recall who chose the wine, but it was chosen – perhaps by providence it chose us – and on first sip it was a jammy snog of flavours: oaky, spicy, vanilla-laced, a silken slip on the tongue. It caused tantalising tremors in all ten toes. We declared ourselves lovers of M'hudi, announcing it a favourite wine of all wines and the only one we would share over dinner at the Lodge. We may have emptied their supply. Intent on drinking M'hudi for the rest of the trip we left Pilanesberg and set off towards Cape Town. The journey between the two cities was not without dramatics, but that's something to come back to.

In Cape Town, we stayed at The Grey Hotel on 49 Napier Street – the nucleus of the De Waterkant region. The various on-site drinking and eating saloons at The Grey Hotel were entitled: The Piano Bar, Lucky Bao, Skybar and Shio. Though known for their epic wine selection, none of these saloons stocked nor had heard of M'hudi, only adding to its mystique.

Do not be fooled by its banner, The Grey Hotel holds the warmest, most colourful of welcomes. A Victorian house in the bullseye of the gay district, it boasted an extraordinary cocktail menu; a rooftop plunge pool with backdrop of Table Mountain; panoramic views of the city; hidden crannies; and a robust roster of live music. Though the hotel's slick rectangular exterior was painted grey, its vibe and vivaciousness was double rainbow with a chrome filter.

Of course, in between our searching for M'hudi, we wedged in a gallimaufry of leisure activities. It would have been barbarous not to have explored the Mother City's huge harvest of cultural treats and bustling social life. And how completely cherishable to have several days unattached to shows and unfixed from schedules, to sprawl out and bumble. We shopped in the tourist malls down by the quay – truckled to the appeal of returning with gifts. You purchased an Obama cooking apron as a present for AE (she'll be back) and I picked up swanky pineapple swimming shorts and gaudy socks. We sweated so much that day, buckets, broke your step count record hiking up the Lion's Head, legs like elastic stretched too far, but boy did we see some sights and moisten the air with innuendo. The sun, you said, yellow as gorse flower – or perhaps that was me.

Sweating in African heat felt so much healthier than sweating back home in Scotland. For someone svelte, smooth-surfaced, light on body and facial hair, I can perspire prodigiously. In my days of working in offices I was no stranger to ploughing tissue under my shirt for extra absorption, limiting my movements to camouflage leakage, and the odd armpit blowdry in the loos. To you, however, this was small potatoes; you sweated magisterially, like a thirsty cheese plant in a tropical garden. I had seen you sweat through a thick denim shirt and outdoor blazer in a tepid Scottish spring. Here under the bleaching heat of one of the hottest countries in the world, you glistened, wore it like a glaze. I'm blowing smoke up your arse but rightly so. Because of you I embrace my sweat.

The hip locals guffawed and snorted when we told them our top activity was visiting Cape Town's Two Oceans Aquarium, but they've not seen the pictures of us in shorts and T-shirts in front of a green-screen-projected image of the bottom of a tropical ocean. I photographed you photographing clownfish, you photographed me photographing jellyfish, and our collective sentiments on the pungent aromas of penguin shit were pure poetry. It sounds silly, trivial in the context of all the musical and literary virtuosos we've engaged with, jejune in comparison to the important conversations we've unpacked in moments of extreme still, but I wouldn't trade that photo for a sultan's fortune. In fact, us coquettish cads opted for the full tourist giftpack: two framed images, two postcards and two keyrings – a mix of green-screen backgrounds featuring sharks, angelfish, octopuses, giant turtles and the bowel-busy penguins.

Those October nights, staying at The Grey Hotel, are at the epicentre of my happiness, in the dearest district of memory. It would be macabre to list the extremities I would go to, the tribulations I would endure, to revisit them. Not so grey a conversation.

Before departing South Africa, we skirted around a plethora of booze bazaars and wine emporiums looking for the magic M'hudi Pinotage potion. We, too, asked a friend in Johannesburg for aid in the search. Sadly, all our questing was in vain.

———

21 July 2018

When people leave, we that remain are left to battle with unanswered questions – some are recondite and specific, others coltish and pithy. For example, it occurs to me walking out the door of Curfew that the version of the tale I decanted upon you about Bill's acquisition of this unique property contains errors. Yes, I believe it still involves him rallying towards the North Pole with a celebratory Elvis statue and, upon return, hastily purchasing Curfew (without ever having visited it) to house a gigantic book of stories that it is hoped will last a thousand years or more. Yet, having heard him tell the tale performatively and in full, I've unearthed new detail and old inaccuracies I wish to correct.

Not to be able to adjust the factuality of this story irks me. But just for a moment. It is piddling compared to the way we constantly evolve life's big events, restorying and reinterpreting under the zeitgeist of our time. Delivering a tweaked rendition of this tale is not the root of the bother, I get that and put my grumble to bed. Besides, somewhere outside today's walk is calling.

———

Alongside a few lustrous humans (Hollie, KB, JB), I was invited back to South Africa in February 2018. This was part of a British Council artist showcase coinciding with the Cape Town Art Fair. I promised you I would return with a trophy bottle of M'hudi. But when I was there, once again, all my shopping trips fell foul, the bounty still mysteriously unfindable.

I upped the ante.

Through the power of social media messaging, I secured our troupe a wine tour of the M'hudi Farm. It was in the famous Stellenbosch region and only forty-five minutes in an Uber from the apartment we were staying in at Green Point. There would be no Table Mountain or Cape Point today, I announced to my fellow travellers, it was to be a *Maaaaahooodddddaaaay*.

Communications with the wine farm had been garbled, suspiciously laconic and devoid of any real detail except for a time and an address and a question as to whether we would like snacks. I took on the offer of snacks and enquired of the price. They noted it would be R150 per person and that the sum included all drinks and edibles. This is only about £8 but I presumed there would be plentiful extras and I couldnae huv gie'in two fucks; I was in all the way and wanted the full treatment.

Our driver had a difficult time sourcing the location of M'hudi – he accidentally ended up in a rowdy township, becoming quickly nervous. Whereas the surrounding vine-yards and wine-tasting centres exhibited flashy signs, exotic plant-life and water fountains, we were looking for two shabbily painted white posts with a rusted iron gate leant against them.

We found M'hudi Towers just before our driver threw in the towel and declared the journey void. Down the bottom of a long unkempt driveway, a head poked out from some wiry bushes to greet us. We were summoned indoors into a massive open-plan living space, super minimalist with a waning grandeur.

Rae-Leigh introduced herself – our maître d' and compere, and the owner of the head that had appeared through the shrubbery. She wore a glamorous frock with an unnerving permanent smile and pointed to a table laid out with glasses and wine. Despite looking the part, she wasn't overly forth-coming about the wines and seemed to draw a blank on any of the questions we had. She was super nice, but her dearth of knowledge was baffling and retorts like 'I usually just drink it' revealed this was her first time hosting. That and her uttering of 'I don't normally do this.'

We were a giggly bunch by the end of the tasting, Rae-Leigh having emptied about six bottles on the four of us. One of the team was especially giggly, having suckled on some cannabis oil left in our flat by an eager partygoer. The giggling became unbeatable as we set each other off into a Catherine wheel of chortling. Rae-Leigh stared on with an unflinching pleasantness. I was already thinking, I can't wait to tell you about this.

Thankfully, our choir of goofiness was interrupted by the arrival of Rae-Leigh's father-in-law, the co-founder of M'hudi Wine Farm. He implanted into us a quick history lesson and declared this to be the first black-owned wine farm in South Africa – the Rangaka family were pioneers. Before acquiring the farm, Rae-Leigh's father-in-law (Diale Rangaka) had been a professor at a university north of Johannesburg and her mother-in-law (Malmsey Rangaka – M'hudi's CEO) had been an accomplished clinical psychologist.

They had procured the farm in 2003 with no real wealth or experience of the wine industry. The deposit was paid for with their pensions and a bond over their home. It was a leap of faith in a plot of land that produced modest amounts of grapes and guava in what would be described as a 'shoddy' slice of the famous Stellenbosch region.

The name 'M'hudi' was derived from the Setswana word *Mohudi*, meaning 'Harvester'. A novel of the same name was written by Sol Plaatje and published in 1930 – it was the first novel to be published by a black African in English. It was in fact finished ten years earlier but Plaatje struggled to find a publisher.

Mhudi is a great and influential African story that sees a bold woman flee her village to restart her life in turbulent, unfamiliar surroundings. It's a story of courage in searching for a new beginning and still seen to have resonance in South Africa today. The author, whose picture hung above us in the tasting room, insisted the book be filed as romance literature.

Fuck me sideways, what an interesting wine to have a tryst with. Up until this point, the story of Beaujolais Nouveau reigned supreme, for me, in terms of a wine with a riveting backstory. It has been dethroned.

We learnt that over the period of 2009 to 2014 M'hudi was soaring – they had won a contract with Marks & Spencer that saw their stock take to the shelves of two hundred stores. They could be found in retailers in the US, Germany, Switzerland, Sweden and Nigeria. Now in 2018, the pair indicated that the future of the company was currently under discussion and the time neared for M'hudi to be passed onto the younger generation. Alas, the M&S contract is no more and their inter-national output has dwindled, but the young team have pushed through a design revamp and are toying with neoteric ideas and outlooks.

That said, Rae-Leigh noted they rarely got visitor enquiries and so mine was accepted as much out of intrigue as anything. They wanted to get to the bottom of how a cohort from Scotland found themselves drinking M'hudi and had developed such a crush on the wine that they would plot a visit to the farm. I told her about us in the Lodge, and our rapacious appetite for the bottle's charms. She asked why you weren't here and I explained you were currently touring America singing songs. She looked sufficiently impressed. We glommed together in this moment, although you never knew it.

At this point Diale marshalled himself off as, apparently, he had a tendency to give away too much wine and the guests were often still there in morning – slurring, singing or passed out. Old six bottles Rae-Leigh it seems was the stingy one – Jiminy Cricket!

A searching glance was exchanged between Rae-Leigh and the grapes outside. She snapped back to the present with an announcement that it was time for the snacks. We were coaxed towards an outdoor dining area and sent off with a bottle of fizzy rosé to keep us company during the short wait. By this point the sun was beginning to dip, dipping but still boasting that hot fuzz that bubbles over landscapes when caught in the net of a temperature soaring. It was then I realised things can have all colour burnt out of them yet still be decked with life.

It turned out snacks meant a big bastard of a banquet – bread, salad, meat and cheese, alongside all manner of salted and pickled picky bits. We got a mousey warning about a couple of scoundrel dogs roaming around and that the bigger one – an American pit bull – tended to push the little one around.

As we quaffed back fizz and scoffed the delicious offerings, I started to feel nervous about our buyer's expectations. It seemed to have been a while since they hosted guests and the shrinking profits of M'hudi were made obvious to us. Second to that, they'd thrown a lavish amount of food and booze at us for a paltry £8 a head. Other wine farm tours and tastings seemed to be up to ten times this price and I'm not sure they decanted anywhere near to the couple of bottles per heid we'd been graced with. I feared they had falsely guesstimated that we represented an alliance of buyers and were, as such, in possession of the profit-making panacea to their current lull. Their new M&S-style saviour. I shared my enervating notion with my fellow merry-makers, who too became a little perturbed. Everything had grown eerie and was beginning to feel like a R. L. Stine *Goosebumps* novel.

With a slaver, a yelp and a needy whimper, a wee baw-faced fluff ball of a dog called Corky clattered through our pensive quiet. He was welcomed in with a playful tickle and a couple of treats from the table. Corky's joie de vivre settled concerns and gave our giddiness another inning on the diamond. One of our collective grew particularly smitten with the mutt, coddling Corky's face in his hands and making baby jazz noises.

We were presented with wine order cards and given a puff to think it over. In that moment we heard another sound – a throaty growl triggering the percussive beat of paws, heavy on the blanched grass. A bigger, more indurate-looking dog came powering our way. Our sated state left us sluggish in reaction and before we could say, 'Jesus fuck, that's a beastly canine,' the American pit bull had removed Corky from under the table like tearing the wrapper off a sweetie.

He then proceeded to viciously and vociferously rape poor Corky as we watched with mouths agape and stomachs turning. The pit bull pounded away, snarling at wee Corky's neck and ears for what felt like an eternity. Our posse swiped towards the pit bull to no avail – the fucker was locked in, more likely to tear flesh than unhook his cock from Corky's arse. We couldn't have chainsawed him off.

We saw Rae-Leigh by shadow first and then her figure followed. Hark, our liberator had come to end this odious violence. But naw, not so fucking easy. Rae-Leigh let loose a crackly chuckle and mouthed softly, 'Oooooh, he's teasing him again.' She then enquired whether we'd decided what wines we wanted – an insouciance commanding her style. We handed the cards over dumbstruck, which took the sting out the anticipation of whether our order numbers were going to appease team M'hudi.

I will be succinct on the moments after. The number of bottles we ordered were the maximum we could afford and the family appeared thankful for it. I made sure Hollie, KB and JB all left with their own liquid nest egg. Rae-Leigh and Diale, who had returned, seemed invigorated by our interest in their story and gave us a scintillating send-off. Despite being in the grassy suburb of the Stellenbosch district we miraculously lassoed a passing Uber back into the city.

In our apartment, we popped a fizzy M'hudi, waxed and beautified the day before going out for a grand finale feast. As for poor Corky's plight, it had ended when we left the table but none of us could shake the feeling the ride that lay ahead for him would be a rocky one. Whether one among us still hears his call echo in their dreams I can't be certain – but when a soft expression swamps over that someone's face, a glass is raised to wee Corky.

As to Rae-Leigh's categorisation of 'teasing' for a brutal raping from a rampant American pit bull, the mind boggles. Teasing?! It was a massive pit bull cock up a minim soft Corky crevice, his body slammed down upon the concrete and pummelled with snarls and bites on the ear. Teasing, sure, fucking teasing!

That aside, in February 2018, I had fulfilled a promise to a beloved pal. Although I would keep this secret from you for the time being.

Come the start of March 2018, I'm two weeks home from South Africa and you're forty-eight hours back from a jumbo US tour. Home for us both now was Glasgow – me in the west end and you in the east; you a veteran, me a newbie, spurred on to move here from Edinburgh by the thought of an increasing number of impromptu get-togethers.

We arranged to meet for dinner at a place called Paradise – a Persian restaurant on Great Western Road. I loafed outside, enthusiastically early, until you appeared all scrumptious with a wide-mouthed grin. As we're seated you mention, 'Oh I think this place might be BYOB.' I let the comment wash off, trying to conceal my effervescence, though I must have blushed with delight. It was likely you'd scanned the menu online before we selected the eatery – we always did our culinary due diligence. I muffled, 'Oh yeah, it's okay, I've picked up a bottle,' then spurted out a follow-up question to keep you off the scent.

We were endowed with menus and began perusing the choices, eyes busy on the dishes, until you placed the card down coolly, peered over at me and mouthed wryly, 'You haven't?! The M'hudi?!' I'm not sure if I was beaming too smugly or flavoured the air with my eagerness, but you guessed it. I scrambled into the bag and up popped a bottle, placed upon the table like a medal; like an old friend you thought you'd never see again – lust evolving into love. You giggled jubilant as an underdog race winner, and instantly it was worth every inch of the arduous trek I began recounting. My face flamed in pride, we chinked glasses, goblets full, grinning into a triumphal arch.

That night, once more, we painted our lips with M'hudi – liquid enzymes for life's great braai.

Dinner was you being yourself and me being mine. We discussed everything we'd achieved but focused on the still to come. I was always left humbled by how matter-of-fact you could be about what other people would call 'your greatness', whittling it down to hard work and honed process. We agreed that neither of us had written nearly enough – songs or poems – and were worthy miles away from becoming a version of ourselves that we fully admired.

I had another bottle of M'hudi in a gift bag I gave to you to take home. No, no, you said, keep it with you and we'll make sure we have it together when the time is right. You were fantastic at bringing back goodies and trinkets, a full fruitage from your trips abroad. This time, however, it had been my turn, and (I must say) I'd excelled. Before we headed our separate ways, we plotted questing back to South Africa and fetching enough M'hudi to fill a lido. Later that night, I put my excess rand aside for this very purpose.

I kept the empty bottle of M'hudi we drank at Paradise. Before I came to Curfew, I took it to the marina where you were found. I weighted it with sea-glass and made of it a bibelot. I wrote a postcard to you and curled it inside – you were a firm believer in sending postcards. The last one I sent you was from Berlin in April 2018 – an arty Polaroid which had a massive Royal Mail 'couldn't gain access to the building' sticker smashed across its face by the time it reached you. The ones you sent me were better thought-through and remain pictorially intact.

Hollie gave me the M'hudi she brought back from South Africa (having been strongly encouraged to purchase as much of their corpus as could be carried) to take to Curfew. The intention was for the wine to be taken in small sips over the month, sparking stories along the way. She gave me hers so as the one in the bag in Glasgow intended for you could remain untouched. Nobody would wish such a thing wasted, although likely I'll not know when or how to drink this final bottle for a moonbeam of years.

———

22 July 2018

I've been waiting for the night sky to show its rancour; tonight it does. So I buckle in, push the bed to the window on Curfew's top floor, and dissolve into the thunder.

Downstairs a door bites at its hinges, bric-a-brac topples and clouds curdle as the lashing wet drowns any sound of town. The darkness, so clasped to its emptiness, is rich and full with the shrieking sinews of wind. In my mind, Curfew is not the focal point of Cushendall but a forgotten outpost; not latitude or longitude but a space station facing off against asteroids from a distant galaxy.

Tonight's sky circus might bring down the satellites, or snap a star off its string. It is fuming fierce enough to question many things thought stable. I think about my best storms – so thick and sheer they're deemed ungodly, those that paralysed a city or bade a river burst its banks. There's one storm in particular, weather that came to our aid when we needed it the most. It was, of course, of African descent.

———

You and I had agreed that one of the highlights from the South Africa trip was in fact something we didn't do, or rather something we shirked out of. Some might say by divine intervention, summoning the great kraken in the sky, others simply by a timely force majeure. Either way, I've never laughed like this.

On docking down in South Africa, we were swift into its bustle. Still acclimatising to the wild west thrills and fast frissons of Johannesburg, it was straight for an exhibition of your illustrations and complementary performance. This was hosted in a gallery called Hazard that occupied the site of an old industrial-style hotel (The Cosmopolitan) in Joburg's lively Jeppestown district. Hazard's founder, Jonathan, was a friend and our South African guide. His business partner, Jonathan noted singingly, came from a wealthy Jewish family that were major players – fingers in pies in both the corporate catwalk and the fecund arts scene. The people to know. In fact, they owned the foundation (NIROX) where we'd be next appearing.

NIROX Word Festival featured artists from all over Africa and nearly every other continent. We tumbled straight into a reading from the writer-in-residence, Athol Williams, who marked himself a poet and a social philosopher and, having recently won the Sol Plaatje Award, attracted worthy purrs of appreciation from the audience. We, of course, didn't know the significance of Sol Plaatje or his novel *Mhudi* at this juncture. I slurped back Athol's words of welcome and headed off to meet The Oyster Lady they had booked in especially for us – a grand gesture that tells you a lot about the festival. Champagne and oysters, wines of a particular vintage and plenty of self-assured chaps in sun hats who worked in finance with investments on the side.

At the head of the family who owned the park was Adie, an exceptionally accommodating host. Adie's youngest son co-ran Hazard Gallery with Jonathan. The fainéant prince of the pack, he was convivial, never giving too much away during our time in his company. The eldest son, the scion of the family, was a charmingly bombastic investment boffin – at least that's the way we profiled him. We called him Fancy Pants. Slash-and-burn, we surmised he showed prowess in taking the scalpel to the least interesting members of any gathering, cutting away time-wasters with ruthless éclat.

He had luscious long hair, mottled brown, tied in a top knot or rather a top cone. His strong arboreal arms clad in beads and bracelets. He wore a buttoned-down white cotton shirt of noticeable quality, pinstripe shorts and boat shoes.

You and I discussed how magnificently hirsute he was – stray fawn tails fell loose from the nest atop his head and his chest hair looked strong enough to string a harp. We concurred that you could make a fantastic pillow from his stuffing. Although he would sometimes seek to appear tatterdemalion, he would always smell great, with an unconquerable immune system and a resplendent glow. Bet he has a pet lion, we intuited; he was more like a lion than some of the other big cat species. We wouldn't blame a lion for desiring him. Yes, in fact, he had most definitely made consensual love to a lion, which roared in rapturous gratification on receipt of his long licentious strokes.

Fancy Pants, entirely indifferent to our existence, unloaded upon us a few fast questions, which we answered as assertively as we could. By the time his third prompt came along he was no longer listening for a response, instead machinating his next conversational kill and reminding himself of his aptitude for making money off both the rise and demise.

We readied ourselves to be torn asunder, and so it came. Fancy Pants left us with an unctuous testimony of words: I'm so happy you guys are here; it's a real honour; let's make sure to hang out. He knew that we knew he'd baulk if we contacted him – he'd already forgotten our names, and that was perfectly okay; in fact, it was as it should be.

Our favourite part of the NIROX was actually breaking out of the park. Jonathan, having been a former resident and an extended part of the empire, was afforded certain privileges.

One of which was commandeering a souped-up golf buggy from the owner's stash. Jonathan loaded us and his brood (who had been roving feral up until this point) into the vehicle and we blasted out the boundaries of the park.

It was our first taste of South African wilderness, wide-open, arid desert, with red dust roads and inexplicable bosky dollops. Being amongst the bright young things of Joburg meant almost having forgotten about the vastness that lay just beyond the breach. We were suddenly alert to the sound of animal calls and the kaleidoscopic effect of the sun on a cooked landscape. Within minutes we'd passed a herd of impala and then the buggy skidded to a stop as a pack of zebra staked claim to the pathway. 'Aye, just stalled here for a second because there's a herd of zebras crossing,' you said to me liltingly. We'd saved the last swig of our dust-topped lagers for a moment like this – tapped the plastic rims and swallowed the lot.

Soon after returning to the festival grounds, we cut the mic on the sprawling double-day stint at NIROX Word Festival and Jonathan piled us into his chariot – a golf-ball white 1984 Mercedes-Benz W123; a tank of a car. After a run of shows plus the handshakes and hugs of a jillion new acquaintances, we had wanted nothing more than room service and house robes. An opportunity to sharpen up our imaginations for the crusades that would soon be coming our way.

On the drive back, we chased eventide towards The City of Gold as Jonathan's sons clambered over us recounting their tales of conquest and collisions. We sank low into the seats ready to switch into holiday mode.

As we breached the congested roads that led into the city, Jonathan suddenly piped up: 'Oh one thing I meant to mention actually, there's a dinner and drinks soirée tonight that Adie's sons are hosting with some of the glitterati and sponsors. Bit of a VIP closing party and you guys are the guests of honour. It's at Adie's eldest's restaurant actually, one of his side projects. So let's nip back to your hotel, a quick change, then we'll hit the town.'

The news hit us like a human head might an anvil. From torpor to imbroglio, hunter to carrion, a sudden riot of mistrusts pissed from eyes – there might be a structured seating arrangement; it would be a very drawn-out affair; what if for larks they did that seat swapping 'hing between courses!

With the urgency of a lit match, you and I exchanged a drastic stare, asserting something had to be done. Yet with you in the front and me in the back we were tactically neutered, unable to confer.

Kind-hearted, benignant Jonathan might call us guests of honour, but Fancy Pants (at least the version of him that married up with the sobriquet we'd created) would see us as pesky gatecrashers. Interlopers from the kiddies' table all up in his dining chamber! He might feed us to his horny lion!

In the coal pits of our own minds we dug for amiable excuses, knowing fine well we had mere minutes until the intended hotel's 'quick change'.

And then came a sound from the now vinaceous sky – a throaty hawk, a crack as if a pebble had hit the windscreen. The crack was followed by another; the firmament rumbled fractious.

Within the time it might take for Fancy Pants to unshackle his cone knot and shake out that mane, we were bombarded from above. A full-on theatre of thunder and lightning.

Jonathan slowed the vehicle as the deluge lashed down. We had sensed something wasn't right as Jonathan twisted in his seat, noticing then the windscreen of the old Mercedes-Benz was fully obfuscated, opaque as a bathroom door. Jonathan thumped the car to an abrupt stop in the emergency service lane.

'Christ on a bike, this happens sometimes,' he informed us. The old wipers on the '84 Benz were prone to seize up and would remain on strike until a mechanic's intervention. After a speedy debrief, the plan concocted was to stick our heads out the windows and collectively shepherd the motor back to the hotel, only a couple of miles away.

As many voyagers had now abandoned their journeys, our passage home proved doable. At the entrance to our hotel a valet in a rain poncho signalled us up the steep incline into the multi-storey carpark. 'Get yourself up to level ten,' he bellowed, 'and go easy, this storm is going to bring the city to a standstill. Hope you've not got anywhere to be! Oh and sweet ride, my friend,' he puffed as a closing gesture.

As instructed, we alighted the vehicle on level ten. By which point the storm had pretty much engulfed the city, uprooting various unidentified objects and flinging them into orbit; dark shapes blasting by, the shriek of smashing glass. Car alarms could be heard screaming beneath the fury of the downpour. So stentorian were the elements, we couldn't hear each other speak. After a quick and feckless fiddle with the wipers, our huddle ran for the safety of the elevators.

'Unfortunately, I think Zeus is telling us to stay put for the night,' Jonathan announced. The rain still stinging the cheeks of our drenched heads, you and I exchanged a glance expressing our delight with this conclusion – a contretemps for Jonathan, a fucking fairy-tale ending for us. Soaked through in the sauce of life, wicked and invigorated we headed for the parlour.

Within an hour, Jonathan and his brood were cuddled up watching a movie in their newly acquired room. You and I were out on our adjoining balconies sporting the leopard-print robes we'd been eyeing up since arrival.

The storm entered its ninth symphony – its clangorous growl and snarling winds came by crescendo and glissando. After clinking cans – we'd thought the occasion worthy of raiding the mini bar – we erupted into fulsome laughter, collapsing into hysteria like we were releasing something trapped inside. A mad, ecstatic laughter that could only come out in such extremities.

Stranded in the centre of a massive city: stormed-in! Fucking brilliant. Our paralysing laughter trucked on for some thirty minutes, intersected by little sprouts of sentences detailing satirical reports of the cancelled party. We held it together only long enough to powder our contentment with a new farcical element of the 'what could have been' dinner and then dissolved back into laughter.

Our faces still throbbed at the breakfast buffet the following morning.

———

You truly were the best person to slink out of stuffy parties with, the only one who appreciated the full scope of a successful escape as much as I did.

More than missing dinner, eating dinner with you, sharing dishes and stories, cocooned in, is the thing I will miss most of all. Just me and you and scran and sincerity and silliness and smut. We have eaten Italian, Japanese, Chinese, Vietnamese, Scottish, French, Indian, Australian, Thai, Nepali, Spanish, South African, Khmer, Mexican, American, German, Persian and at many specialist hipster fusion joints. A German scientist working with gorillas in the Congo has discovered that these great apes hum and tunefully exhale while eating, composing hoppity food songs. Via euphonic noise-making, and body percussion, we did the very same – composed mealtime melodies. Dinnertime has been an awful lot quieter since you left.

23–24 July 2018

Upon departing Curfew, each visiting artist must leave behind a trace of themselves – something beyond fingernails and eyelashes, beyond replenished spices, a refilled gas canister or their height scratched into the door frame.

I elect to buff up Curfew's cosy yet august library of books by donating my well-thumbed version of *The Rain in Portugal* by Billy Collins. It's a winner all around – stanzas that could charm the pants off a reluctant reader, and not too unnerving for someone braced for a period of solitary confinement. But it's not just Billy; I made this copy bespoke – attaching to the inside cover a poem I wrote for you as a way of saying cheerio. I resolve not to read this one again; its voice will live in *The Rain in Portugal*, listening to the rain in Cushendall.

With the book smug on the shelf, it's time to leave Curfew's sanctum. I've measured the distance from The Grey Hotel to The Curfew Tower in units of missing and loving. The eight months between laying my head down in our Cape Town abode and making a nest of these antique bricks appear more as an epoch of understanding than a linear passing of time.

And so, to me, The Curfew Tower and The Grey Hotel are twinned in the way cities, towns and counties are twinned. I may be the only one to have made such a correlation and thus will contact the Intercontinental Twinning Association to homologate this match. I believe Curfew's keeper has an 'in' with the ITA.

What's clear is that I'm reluctant to heave the anchor up, come out of my Tower's mooring. I've spent 90 per cent of my time here on my own and not a day has gone by where I've not written or thought about you for hours – no qualms about it, nae danger.

We did not watch *Withnail & I*, stray too far nor frequent any of the watering holes. But I did visit you with a depth, divinity and dedication that is not possible in the routine of my Scottish city living.

Through Curfew's mucky windows my mind has flown. Voyaging into stories of childhood and the friendships that sculpted me – love's losses and life's murky lessons. I've slept not with sight of stars but with their sensation, which, in some ways, proved better than the stars themselves.

I will soon be crossing ocean, from Northern Ireland back to my intimate Scottish anchorage. I hope my vessel is seaworthy. I hope my head is ready for the hush and plunge of familiar sociality; I hope my courage holds firm. After a month cradled in Curfew, I am ready to visit where you left us.

2

Come What May into June

2 May 2018
Edinburgh / Glasgow, Scotland

We agree. You'll be coming on this road trip with me and Hollie in two days' time and, nope, not impinging, not one bit – I love you too. We'll stay at The Tavern in Croon. Yes, it's a great spot, no wonder such a profusion of songs and poems have been penned here. Many curious creatures thermal the sky over Croon; it has a mythic ring to it.

So it's a Croon opening and for the second night we've pencilled in a visit to The Lengths in Achaflute – a house-cum-studio-cum-retreat overseen by friends of ours. The future, after that, is up for grabs in every single way; the trip's choreography still to be set. The plan espoused is simply to travel together, our compass pointing north beyond the Scottish central belt.

This same day, a brim-full article is ushered my way by a journalist from the Scottish Provincial Press – it is an interview and images to light a fuse for the event you and I will do to close the Ullapool Book Festival this coming 12 May. Your cover illustration of the oyster takes centre page and makes me recall when you asked how vulvic the cover oyster should look and that I said six out of ten. I think you opted for an eight; some libidinous sorts have even ranked it nine. Either way, oysters and fannies remain two of my favourite things to explore with the mouth.

Around about this time, you did an interview for Google and told me to watch it. This was unusual for you – you never drew me to such forums. In the interview, you narrate how you approached the book and made a declaration of doing the next one together – this was always the plan.

I was right excited about Ullapool: a great place name, a great distance away and the location of one of my first family holidays. From my Ullapool debut at seven, I remember the sharp wind and salty bite of the sea air. I alas also recall the assassination of my new best holiday friend – a one-armed crab named Wullie. The culprits were my older sister and her cartel of killers (Emma and Sara), who had excluded me from their games. Quickly becoming miffed the ostracisation wasn't hitting me hard enough on account of my new crustacean friend, they machinated an attack. I was lured away for a stone-skimming competition, leaving Wullie unguarded and defenceless. They seized the opportunity and flattened Wullie with a rock, her organs smooshed across the sand like spilt jam on a new carpet.

This coastal execution is my earliest fully formed memory. I have flashes of older memories told through toddler's eyes, but these are mudded stock, inconsistent and fragmented. Each time they look a little more like a photograph, and a little less like what my mind backed up all those years ago. The clumsy cover version of a song that hums away in the background of a cheap restaurant, recognisable only by its anthemic chorus. This memory of Ullapool, however, is different. From the cockpit of my mind it can be landed safely on the runway time and time again. Upon us being invited to Ullapool Book Festival, I recounted this story to you and was treated to your sympathies.

Ullapool was to go on to host three other salient happenings for me:

i a show as part of Neu! Reekie!'s *Anywhere But the Cities* tour in 2015;

ii a group activity trip, whereby it served as a stop-off en route to climbing the magical mountain of Suilven in 2016; and

iii accompanying Hollie to her event at Ullapool Book Festival in 2017 – day-tripping to Durness in the gap.

The perfect treble whammy of precursors before heading up to Ullapool ourselves – the *Oyster* boys, fully fluid at UBF 2018.

Suilven, which is around three miles from Ullapool, is not to be so blithely skipped past. This kenspeckle mountain is a well-known shape-shifter. From some angles, it can look like a huge bull seal raising his body off ground as if ready to brawl. From other angles, it's an abrupt rocky nipple. It surges up from within bogs and moorland and makes itself known for miles around. Suilven is formidable, treacherous and forbidding if taken off guard. Yet for those who choose the right path, exhibit patience and tread kindly, it is a most accommodating host. It might be just shy of Munro status (3,000 feet-plus) but what it lacks in height it makes up for in swagger. The great poet Norman MacCaig has a poem entitled 'Climbing Suilven', which ensures the mountainous hunk is venerated amongst young scribes. Seek it out.

My Ullapool voyage with you would have been my fifth time there; it had all the makings of a precious trip, the front prong of a gold crown. I would have suggested scaling Suilven once more. I would have been sent packing, negotiated down to Ullapool Hill, which, let's face it, would have been far more enjoyable.

4 May 2018
Edinburgh to Croon, Scotland

A 15.00 departure time is fixed, the road trip's naissance. And seeing as it's light 'til late, this is equivalent to an a.m. set-off in the winter season – a similar number of hours of sunlight left for exploring under. Croon we know for sure is our initial destination. The rest is a dream still to be dreamt.

You meet Hollie and me at the end of George Street and we amble towards her motoring-vessel. You inform me you have finally capitulated and began to watch the hit series *Vikings*, which I have been quietly advocating and you resisting. I am not a huge fan of the show and you are not massively averse to it either; this tug of war is merely jocular – *Vikings* the rope's heave-ho.

You describe *Vikings* as the last sausage roll at the buffet. To which I retort by all appearances, yes – but take the greedy plunge and get ready to be rewarded. The filling-to-pastry ratio is spot on, the warm flakes crumble well, and some cunt has had the common courtesy to leave the brown sauce out, which, if slathered over the pastry, will become as valuable as icing on cake. We often spoke in food analogies when toying with TV – just a couple of gherkins on the great charcuterie board of life.

It was the appearance of The Seer that kept you watching *Vikings*. I'm unsurprised it was the oracular over the brawls that finally drew you in.

Hollie's motoring-vessel now wears a behemoth bike rack of which both you and I take fun. But not too much as the rack remains empty, for her new beauty of a bike got chored from an outer Cambridge train station just days after she excitedly procured it. Cambridgeshire is pretty much the bottom biscuit in the pack in terms of serious crime, yet it's at the *ne plus ultra* of GTB (grand theft bicycle). Hollie's understandably upset about the thieving but remains a cone full of joyousness as a road-trip companion.

As we set off, I produce a snack of carrots, which you decline. Although you do inform me that carrots release more goodness when cooked than eaten raw; you say the carotene in them comes out to play. I deem this useful information and plan constructive changes to my cooking regime.

The first stop is unplanned, barely out of Edinburgh, in a scenic village in Fife (its southernmost settlement). Hollie has to do a telephone interview and can't conduct this confidently whilst driving and being made a spectacle of. We invest our time wisely and scamper up a teeny wee lighthouse (most toaty lighthouse I've ever seen). The hexagonal brick structure wears its roof like a beanie hat, atop of which is a slanted cross made of old pipe welded together – a sort of less ostentatious papal tiara. In the building's light gallery is us beaming. It's a tight fit for both these bodies but we embrace it and feel like pilots of a rocket ship all set for take-off. Yes, we're ready to head up above the stratosphere. Yes, we're prepared to come back down by parachute. Right now, the ocean is a wondrous force for bouncing back light; it is milky and dancing with wind. It does not crave our absence.

The call is done, the lighthouse is doted over, sea salt clings to our cheeks and there's a gloop of anticipation building for the road ahead. With us clambered back inside it, the motoring-vessel moves off, passing towns and villages, and delivers us to Croon. We load into The Tavern Inn, and agree, despite the umpteen hotels we stay in every season, checking in some-where for pure pleasure never fails to thrill.

We take tea in a rival hotel. I order the special then switch to steak and onion rings because I like eating in unison with you and this sounds equally appealing. Hollie chuckles because I mostly eat vegetarian when we're together so she and I can share a party of scrumptious dishes rather than dedicate to single plates. I have recklessly abandoned this custom and bunked in with my carnivore buddy.

As intended, we clear the plates and then meet old friends – singers and delicious drink makers – whose company pro-vides the pudding. Roseate, we take our full bellies and flush cheeks home.

This is a collective now, the cast has taken, the joy and jokes we evoke make these weighty bodies lighter on our toes. There's one last tipple at the hotel which is snuck up to the room – you and Hollie natter on the floor; I'm pinballing about the beds then soon asleep. You send me off with a raised 'Miiiiiiccchael' – half laughing at me, half laughing at the ridiculousness of your attempt to instate decorum. You and Hollie clink glasses and chatter further into the star-studded late. I take you both into my dreams, continue the conversation in the mind's unconscious sky.

5 May 2018
Croon to Achaflute, Scotland

You call me brave at breakfast for ordering the smoked kippers and eggs. I take the compliment because it was a risk and not one that would be described as rewarding. We decided you'd be continuing on to Achaflute. You made a subtle enquiry about staying on longer, keen to visit The Lengths. By this point, it was already taken as given that this doesn't end here.

By Croon harbour, we pay a friend from last night a farewell visit – his beau and their crop of kiddies greet us at the gate. Equipped with the knowledge our day-tripping is tarrying, ballooning into a longer adventure, we head down to the harbour front. For the water, four feet strip off their socks and wade in; two feet opt out, skirting around, tickling the chin hairs of the shoreline. Night's erubescence still bathes in our skin.

For our travels we are slung a CD called *Bright Phoebus: Songs by Lal and Mike Waterson*. Our friend thrusts it into your hand afore set-off. The song 'Scarecrow' is extolled to us as the pinnacle pick. We listen to the first run of tracks and concur 'Scarecrow' is the pièce de résistance. However, several voracious guffaws are let loose as some of the more discordant notes seem to stick it out for miles – akin to an off-key harmonica solo that defies the biology of breath in its inordinate length. We are introduced to several protagonists in the album, the likes of Danny Rose and Winifer Odd – the former of whom I garner is knocked down by a tractor. Listening to the album is a befuddling experience within which we take a lot of fun, creating our own sub-stories. Although no doubt Lal and Mike are ingenious songwriters to a more adept ear, it is a perplexing listen for this new passenger.

I am very glad this is the CD we left Croon with as the laughter it draws out of us narrates the afternoon.

Of course, it's House of Bruar for our roadside recess. Located just outside of Pitlochry, House of Bruar is the fanciest stop-off in Scotland, where countless families detonate into argument as kids stake claim to their pricey range of quaffables and scoffables: smoked fish, cured meats and designer chutneys stacked phone-box high. Eat under their glass roof or dine alfresco, and then wander into the section of the store that earned HoB its wings as Scotland's premier independent country fashion retailer: tweeds, cashmere and hunting gear, in that royal-rural style. With its old toys, sweets and seeds, it's both an enchanting grotto of Scottishness and a troubling hurl of over-priced jam(boree). It all depends what the mood is and how much money is in the skyrocket. We are kitted out with nuggets and cheap taste, and so relish it.

As an offering to our next hosts in Achaflute, I scavenge: a medley of olives, garlic and chillies; organic farm eggs; a hunk of fancy-looking rainbow-seeded bread (which really could have hung on a gallery wall); and some Argyll Smoked Mussels (in richly flavoured oil). These sloppy lozenges of wonder are a cracking find – a delicacy we've lauded and enjoyed separately but never together, and so there's a band of excitement belted around us for later. We're that content with the forage it's as if we hauled these molluscs from the nets ourselves.

Wi the messages* done we feed ourselves and go alfresco in the posh cafe. I still feel like a pretend adult here and am bamboozled by not having to justify my purchases to a parent or guardian holding the purse strings. Likely I'd be offering up an increased chore load for the ensuing week in order to push through the sale. I think we all felt the same but remained silent so as not to shatter the sophisticated mien of a 'think nothing of it' House of Bruar shopper. Despite now knowing how to season words like 'bucolic' into conversation, I feel worse behaved than when I took trips to Dobbies Garden Centre with

* This being in the Scots language sense meaning 'the shopping' – the act of fetching grocery off a list from a selection of small stores across town with a nod to messenger boys scooping up items and delivering them to the wealthy or those unable to collect. I think this was more common in Edina than Glasgow but might get a boot in the baws for saying that.

my mum and grandma around the eight- or nine-year-old mark. Garden centres have always been a place where the working classes are on our best behaviour so as not to stand out – or so it felt growing up. It was one place I wouldn't dare act up as I knew how much reputationally was riding on it.

Back at HoB, soup spoons chink ceramic bowls as I gaze into, perhaps, my two favourite people in the world – offering each a sip of my raspberry lemonade to let them know how I feel. This feels more like a birthday lunch, the sugary mouthful proffered in place of a slice of cake. There is a pause in the moment, as if the whole of Scotland is together in an eyes-closed, deep, planetary inhale. A reminder to all personages and puzzle solvers to take note and appreciate their surroundings – an olive branch so as those caught in a huff might reboot into better temperaments.

We set off again towards Achaflute; you and I crash out, bellies bubbling and sun sloshed over us. Not just napping but marinating the evening's conversation. Perhaps Hollie feels a little like a mum driving wee spud and his pal around during the school holidays. Likely not – it's far sexier and more serene than that. Not us sleeping and drooling on ourselves, but the landscape prospering; and the fecundities of friendship that blossom between us.

You slumber on and I rise to a momentous happening, Hollie singing lead on one of your songs (playing through the car speakers). It was a brilliant bubble to be in, all post-nap torpor and oven-roasting slow. She comes in strong on the choruses and key lyrical hooks, then enthusiastically muffles through the verses where the words don't come quick enough. It's like your steaming auntie on the karaoke – bammy but everyone laps it up and feels warmer for having heard her chanting. I love the gallus ones that just go for it under these circumstances, belt it out – resolute to sing with full knowledge it's going to waver from words of triumphant splendour to a patchy warble.

I willed you awake when Hollie was full flow, knowing you'd get a kick out it, but as fortune had it you slept right through this rendition and rose instead to Shakira – another favourite on Hollie's playlist for the breasts small and humble mantra. Fair play, that must have been empowering to many young boob growers the world over.

Some of the finest collections of blood, flesh and bone the great breath-maker ever cocktailed into existence are in my loving grasp. That's how I felt as we drew near to our next destination.

The motoring-vessel cackles to a stop on the gravel outside The Lengths of Achaflute. This is a 1960s rectangular schoolhouse that's been renovated over a number of years into a home, arts workshop, recording studio and sometimes gig venue by Zusie.* The glass front spills itself onto Loch Eil – where wild otters are spotted and many a bonfire doth blaze. The interior is teeming with intriguing items from old medical

* Zusie is the collective term for a team of two sculptor-musicians (individually named Ziggy and Suzie) who have clubbed together to transform an old 1960s Highland schoolhouse into a contemporary bohemian sanctuary.

models to rare records, sought-after whiskies, miscellaneous hand-sculpted objects and a tireless love hound called Bow. I once shagged in their deep-sunk, freestanding copper bath and earned a frivolous telling-off. Despite this, my resident credits are still good at The Lengths.

We consume the Argyll Smoked Mussels. It's noteworthy. We dip and slurp as one – sloppy fingers, ochre liquid spills. It feels almost sacrilegious washing the oleaginous coating off our mitts.

Zusie unveils a McClaggan thirty-seven-year-old single malt, sherry cask which you and Hollie take a nip of. Later the next day, you proudly declare it the best whisky you've ever tried. I like this more and more – that exemplary rating, your whisky-tasting apogee, superlative sup.

''Mon throw the ball for Bow' is a teasing crowd pleaser of a remark made every time you slip out for a cigarette. Mon throw the ball. Throw the ball. Throw the ball for Bow. The ball is always bouncing even when you're not. The ball gag punctuates the evening. Bow never tires of fetching, a slave to the chase.

The *Harry Potter* steam train passes by on the other side of Loch Eil and I don't hide my excitement. It is heading to Glenfinnan Viaduct and so it is decided we too will head to the Viaduct tomorrow – Zusie's plotted the route on our behalf and I've calcified the intent. You're dutifully and gleefully in and though not a *Potter* fan you dig an old bridge, and I can tell you don't want the voyage to end yet. We are unanimous in this continuation, no stopping us.

Our travelling coterie are allotted The Lengths' two-bed retreat lodgings. So with the plates scraped clean we dissolve into the dreams that have been waiting patiently for us to fall.

6 May 2018
Achaflute to Mallarn, Scotland

In the morning your snoring vibrates the air like a swarm of bees circling the room. Sun shoots sprout up to the ceiling – ephemeral beams of graffiti from beyond this planet raked over sheets and feet. The snoring is a fuzzy symphony, which takes me straight back to our holiday lodge in South Africa waiting for the dozy tune to crescendo so as I can wake you for a splash in the pool.

I love to swim and am always plotting pools to dip into. You knew this only too well and became trustily familiar with my splash times during our tour of South Africa. In fact, you set up a clandestine group text entitled 'McPeeds', which had a primary purpose of grassing to Hollie about just how many times I cajoled you into photographing me 'dicking about in the pool'. I power on with this sort of play as I think you secretly love it. It gives your big chortling pus the opportunity to adopt the older curmudgeon role.

The day's agenda is visits to the Glenfinnan Viaduct and the Silver Sands of Morar – *Harry Potter* and *The Lord of the Rings* tinged (the latter in lexicon only), but stunning Scottish scenery first and foremost. We might drop you in Mallarn for the afternoon train back to Glasgow, as this was only supposed to be a one-night trip for you, which has grown arms and legs and beating heart. That said, we're only flirting with the concept of curtailing the voyage, a courtesy, and it's not mentioned again.

By 15.15 we've tottered up the National Trust Viewpoint trail and conquered its precipice. We sit down with the summit and, amongst searching strangers, eyeball the viaduct. I replay *Harry Potter* and *Ring of Bright Water* scenes in which this structure starred. Then try to forget them and concentrate on the ancient wonder of it. The grass below is Granny Smith apple green and laid down in front of the stone with all the majesty of marbled flooring. In the shadow of the brick, red and blue dots from the woollen jumpers of tourists pixilate and freckle. The mountains that coorie around the viaduct are darker tones with a well-earned pomposity.

No train passes yet a pair of clouds mesh together to cast a gigantic shadow and, for a flash, the bridge appears as if cursed. The two oval clouds soon separate like a riven pair of bollocks. Loch Shiel trundles into view and the Glenfinnan Monument deigns us with its presence. Even in the overcast, the surrounding shrubbery wears a lapidary coating.

This bridge has been travelled over since 1898 but not by us and that makes no difference at all. You have started the descent; we've all got the picture to look at later. The number of selfie sticks flailing about reaches saturation, so we move out. There is some walking in circuits around the area but no walking on the bridge itself; that's prohibited and has nearly cost a few straying *Potter* zealots more than a grey hair or two.

The Silver Sands are a mere thirty-five minutes from here and the drive passes so quick it's as if the moment moved without us. All gabble and murmur we head west from Glenfinnan. Scotland is fucking incredible and we all agree we should get out of the central belt and into the Highlands much more often. On one side of us is Loch Morar, on the other the North Atlantic Ocean. We gaze over to The Isle of Eigg; a little further off is Rùm. These waters, what lives in them and loops around them, chart a fabulous mélange of colour: silver, periwinkle, mauve, azure, turquoise and royal blue. Our eyes are fine dining on landscape.

There is a boat bobbing in the water by the Silver Sands of Morar called the *Davy Diver*. It's canary yellow and resting but quite the sight just bobbing there. Best of all some chancing fun lover has made a couple of rope swings up top of the sandy banks, which Hollie and I gravitate towards. You perambulate by the water's edge and eventually we meet in the middle.

'Not fancy a wee go on the swing. I'll push ye?' I say.

'I've decided against it – it'll bring me absolutely no pleasure. I don't like the height or the motion. I'm great down here on the sand,' you say.

'Fair enough – at least you've considered it,' I say.

'Never feel guilty about seeking pleasure,' you say.

This sentence came out strong and sure, a totem teaching; as if the allegorical ending to a long story. It connected the dots in my memory of all the times you've spoken this way before

– redolent of more serious intent. So steeped in prescience was the way you mouthed it that I question whether you spoke it out loud or passed it telepathically.

With that settled it is on to Mallarn, where we check into a Highland hotel at the top of a steep road. It is near dinner and so – wasting no time – we book a table swiftly to secure a coveted window spot. An hour later we're seated and shooting the eyes' arrows as far as they'll travel, haughty with our hunger. Outside, Skye is staring back over the water with one of those wry looks that suggests it's about to burst into yodel.

Dinner with you and Hollie. These are palmary moments.

No, I don't regret spending £75 on the seafood sharing platter. Aye, it is a crumb indulgent and you call me a lush (to Hollie's hilarity) but we are twinned in this bonhomie. I do not regret us gorging ourselves on a platter boasting an estimated: forty mussels, sixty prawn tails, six gargantuan langoustines, twelve scallops and a heft of dipping bread – a platter most definitely intended for filling more than two bellies. Of course, there is wine – we would not do a meal such as this the disservice of being without it. The platter is its own constellation; it does not fit on the table, for its circumference is akin to Jupiter, not decommissioned Pluto. You and Hollie have to swap seats so we can battle this formidable foe thigither, in formation.

We are leviathans feasting with and on each other. The messy display attracts nods of reverence from onlookers populating the tables in orbit around us. These nods are a cloud of praise comfortably taken; this comfort in taking praise is far too rare for brilliant you.

Over yonder, the island of Skye sits down to tea with us – we address it in stories and long glances cast over. On Google Maps this water is labelled 'Inner Seas off the West Coast of Scotland' (Atlantic Ocean) – a very formal name for our salty guest, the ghost at the table.

Whilst eating the platter there is a dearth of chatter; it has given way to unwavering dedication. Let it be known this is not portentous – it is the opposite, the gooey vim of not needing chit-chat. We are apples, here's our core, sprouting pips in every belly. Even vegetarian Hollie sooks a mussel down but, *shhhhhhhhh*, don't tell her family or she'll never hear the end of it.

This supper was garlic-butter gorgeous, love on its tiptoes, the last meal we had together and one of your last on this whizzing planet. It isn't quite fit for purpose, but I surmise you'd chip in with: it wasn't far off either.

p.s. yes, we order starters anaw but these were modest and too alluring to let pass by. Thon pudding you shared with Hollie was one step beyond for me but youse looked cherubic splitting it and you were often one step ahead.

p.p.s. by the time the £149.50 (plus £20 cash tip) cleared from my bank account, three days later, you had left us and something had left me; but right there in that moment we were brimful. It was love.

A nearly accurate conversational excerpt from dinner:

Hollie: God I really love your illustrations. They're so beautiful.
What's your favourite thing to draw?

You: (*ponders existence with anchorless ease then stares off to a distant skyline – magic is in this wait, beatitude, cerulean silence slathered in hope*)

It would have to be severed arms. Yeah, severed arms.

I love those wee guys.

Hollie: . . . (*mouth agape*) . . .

You: Also clouds, jolly little clouds. Maybe that's more what you were looking for.

All: . . . (*laughter bubbles from the belly up*) . . .

7 May 2018
Mallarn to Inveraray, Scotland

They fucked up your breakfast order despite you having been there ten minutes earlier than us and having the look of someone in a hurry. (In light of the devastation that awaits, this seems more macabre than it should, nefarious even. It's not, it's simply human error, triviality.) I give you my eggs, which was virtually the same as your intended order and came first. You put up a wee fight, but I come on strong in persuasion and you are fed. I check you have a book for the train – you do, confirming its existence without giving it a label. On the long and beautiful journey ahead of you, words will make braw cabin buddies alongside the views of the Trossachs and Gare Loch. We left on a Friday for one night in Croon and it is Monday in Mallarn. This is the sweater love is knitted from, a patchwork quilt to follow – uncharted, unplanned days wiggling across the great Scottish wilderness / tourist hotspots. This has gone beyond a road trip into the realms of, yes, a true voyage.

Hollie and I are not sure where we're going today, but otters are on the agenda and we'll not be heading home this moon's third quarter. You, reluctantly, board the 10.10 train, having left us with your hug. You are pleased not to be carrying a guitar – that always makes travel more buoyed. I miss you already but will see you in a few days' time in Ullapool.

Somewhere en route south, Hollie and I pass a stopped train resting on the curl on the side of a loch. I think you're on it. I point out the train to Hollie and go to call you on the phone but there's no reception. I would have told you to disembark at the next station, that we now had a plan and you should come to the Scottish Sea Life Sanctuary and then we could drop you down the road after.

Later that day – I guess you're nearing Glasgow – I send you a text message that concerns an otter. A thirteen-year-old arthritic otter called Lewis. He's not a wild one but a resident of the Scottish Sea Life Sanctuary. You liked the picture. Ya fucker. That's what I mean by you liked the picture; it expelled from you a digital text rendition of 'Ya fucker.' To avoid any doubt, reader, this is exclusively celebratory, as in 'Ya Fucker, I've just won £60 on a scratch-card'; and not 'Ya Fucker, you ate my last lychee.' Okay? Good.

After the otters, Hollie and I stop at a forest and then a church on the fringes of Loch Awe (Scotland's most aptly named loch) ending up in a Spa Hotel in Inveraray. We drink in the last of the light in their outdoor Jacuzzi and I fling my thoughts your way. Bubbles on the chest are great and not to be missed; and so Hollie is steadfastly stripping off because no-one is about and her nipples too deserve to be free and shouldn't be imprisoned just because they're bigger and capable of lactating.

Your words ring out in my ears: 'You'll never be more relaxed together than in a spa!' I say it out loud in jest. This is what you told me after a spa trip you'd taken. Did I think this would spur us into getting a luxurious couple's massage at Shepherd's Tree Lodge in South Africa after some rare wildlife spots? You ken what, I certainly wouldn't have ruled it out.

8 May 2018
Inveraray to Glasgow, Scotland

In the morning, Hollie and I stop for oysters by Loch Fyne. I report to you that Hollie sucked the juice out the shell and took a lick of the flesh but no swallow quite yet.

This puckishness accompanied by a full pictorial report entitled 'some stuff we saw'.

Image 1 – sundial on the edge of the world.

Image 2 – churchy courtyard strewn in crisp leaves.

Image 3 – tall trees reaching skywards, growing thinner, taken from supine on the forest floor.

Image 4 – a Bucklebury flamingo balanced on one leg, gazing upon a wood soon to be sexed in.

Image 5 – a big pottery shed for someone keen on pottery.

Image 6 – Hollie with her head poking through a celebratory face-in-the-hole picture board. Depicted on the front there is a painted scene of a boat exploring lochlands. Hollie's head emerges on the body of the captain; above her a slogan is emblazoned: 'We've had an otter-ly great day out at the Scottish Sea Life Sanctuary'. It is genius. As are all otter-based puns: I otterly love you; we otter be together; significant otter; you otter be ashamed of yourself; in otter news; the list goes on.

Image 7 – two giant amethyst beanstalks converging into the gemstone equivalent of a lattice archway. These are housed in Treasures of the Earth – Fort William's gemstone museum – and on second viewing appear considerably more priapic than first thought.

We are coming back to Glasgow to stay with Hollie's gran (Gaga), who is ninety-two years old, a former schoolteacher and a Beach Boys fan. She also fosters covert ambitions to travel back in time and work in Paris as a (high-end) go-go dancer.

From Gaga's loft in Stepps, I watch the sun set on the end of a splendiferous journey. The night sky carries the heat of the coming summer; the wind is easing up. Looking back on the miles travelled – a humble bunch – I've never felt so many human swoons. I scuttle to bed with music trilling inside my chest.

Moments later, just before midnight, I receive an earth-shattering phone call from your kin. In it, the news that you are missing. Some worrying messages appeared on your social media account in the hours before and now thousands are on alert and composing notes of support hoping it's not too late – myself included.

> *I text you;*
> *check your last reported time online*
> *– less than an hour;*
> *I private message you;*
> *too scared to call,*
> *I wait for a reply.*

9 May 2018
Edinburgh and Fife, Scotland

You were last seen leaving a South Queensferry hotel, near the Forth Road Bridge, around 1 a.m. on this the 9 May 2018. You're missing and considered vulnerable.

A requested 7 a.m. meeting with the police confirms the seriousness of your absence. I am in the 'last people to have seen you' category. The ones suspected of holding clues as to your whereabouts.

I rush from Gaga's back to my wee flat, where the police are waiting – something compels me to meet the officers on home turf. As soon as it's over, Hollie and I set off in search of you because no good can come of being motionless during a time like this.

It's still early and yet my feet already throb from the petrifying steps they've taken. I head straight for the little lighthouse in the fishing village we first stopped in – the hotel you left from is walking distance from here and this is where my mind volleys. All dribbles, skin poker hot with the image of us giggling scarfed around me. You're not in the throat of the lighthouse or staring out its great eye. I wonder if that's your breath, a patch shaped like Ireland, on the bulb's glass orb. The ocean is uglier now, turbid and chaotic, a world unknown. I came here because it feels like a full revolution, returning to the beginning. Just a few days back we are on this spot in the undaunted freshness of a trip yet taken.

I learn now this lighthouse is called North Queensferry Light Tower and is the smallest working lighthouse in the world. How did we miss that? Of the two-hundred-plus lighthouses in Scotland this is our littlest sentinel, its luminosity set to balance the tumult of the briny deep – such bravery from one so small is a ballad of hope.

For a while, it's just Hollie and me and the seabirds tossing crab carcasses into the air. We barely pass another human for several fraught hours. The skilful ocean has made enough sea glass to fill a lake in the first hundred metres alone. There is an inferno in my cheeks. It's barely visible to others yet I soon feel its fiery fangs pierce my resolve. This flush enters me when my body goes into panic mode. I am out of my depth.

Everything becomes an omen – in the pop of seaweed underfoot, a prognostication. Immaculate cone-shaped shells spiral into pointing fingers. Any footprint not seconds fresh must be from those that fled these lands long ago.

The heron hunting fish in rock pools knows nothing of this unutterable ache and I would keep it that way. The oyster-catcher, needling the fringes of the sea, is piping out a queer song. I'm not sure if I trust it's truly here.

Helicopters overhead, in their insectile buzz, offer the solace of knowing that higher eyes than ours are scanning land. Machines being sanctioned to search is a tenebrous light.

I find and keep an oyster shell, a stone that resembles a shark's tooth, a smooth brown pebble with tiger-orange flashes – they chute into my pocket. The thunderous sound of you laughing on the balcony above Johannesburg holds my head high. We laughed into a storm and surpassed it. Legs keep moving, there's no cause to stop.

As if on a psychedelic trip I stumble across obscure beach art: a frame made of stones laid out in the sand. Grass layered across the bottom to depict itself on a bigger, grassier scale. A small boulder with hay around it in the top left-hand corner is the sun radiating. A bulbous rock, left of centre, is placed horizontally to become the trunk of a tree, plump as a baobab, Teletubby-hipped. The foliage is made from scorched debris, the remains of a bonfire. It has taken careful time to assemble this scene, concentrated minutes and some farming. I wonder if there's a propitious message to the collage, if it's imbued with secrets. There is a sandcastle nearby that appears shaped by the same careful hands. In detective stories fear and loss are simply part of the narratorial algebra, alongside clues and riddles; the endings almost always satisfy. It's a welcome trope.

We pass the tourist boat tours that offer a range of bird-watching and bridge-viewing trips – also in the evening a salsa dancing cruise.

We pass crows and rabbits. I'm grumbling at the gulls who squawk to the tune of toddler tantrums. There is a bottle of Cava Reserve bolt upright abandoned by the side of a road.

At the end of the day Hollie and I have walked many miles; my body feels like cheap meat chewed down to a gristle, but we will keep grinding on. Inside my skin, jewels are sparkling for you.

Like praying while drunk, I do not think I will find what I am looking for – you, safe and breathing – but am too focused on moving and not giving up to tackle such a colossus. I have never felt so scared as this.

10 May 2018
Lost

There is much more searching and many more miles, but here are the paper-printed facts.

You are last seen walking out a hotel in the direction of the Forth Road Bridge, an unfortunately common suicide spot.

Despite coordinated search efforts and abundant media coverage, you do not come safely home.

Your body is found by a kayaker in the nearby Port Edgar Marina at around 7.30 p.m. on Thursday 10 May. You are pronounced dead shortly after.

You will never come home.

I will study these days like a faith – an inherited religion that never quite fits.

The weather on the day you die is spectacular, expressing itself in sunshine pyrotechnics, ethereal beams and pirouetting shadow. The welkin has something to say; everyone has something to say.

I cannot express how beautiful I found each glimpse of hope that was sent our way.

Thank you for sending them. Thank you for trying. Just, thanks.

3

An Aftermath's Guide to Breathing

By the time you were found, hundreds (into thousands) of people were looking for you; I imagine every one of them will have asked things of themselves they would never repeat. I am no different.

I emerge from the crash bleeding, but still loving, still breathing. It's now a case of survival. That's what comes next. Living while you don't is its own arcane act of endurance. I will remind myself every day, there is no shame in having to try this hard to stay afloat. To keep going is a gift.

I find myself running from the stillness, a mantra of anywhere but home. Heading places just to stay in locomotion, to steer away from the clutch of big decisions. To occupy the mind with basic choices, like: is this my bed / what shall we eat / where can I purchase a toothbrush? To be able to say in return: sorry, I'm not from here / I don't know the way / yes, that's right, I too am lost.

. . .

The day you leave I issue an SOS message to friends in Hong Kong and Italy. They board flights and alert me to their landings. I am lucky to have such nourishment at my beck and call should the circumstances command it. They do, tenfold.

We congregate in Leith by The Shore. Each in this throng

knows you and I want to be surrounded by people of this calibre. One such friend is Bréon, who makes a sudden toast to pull all our separate threads together and hoist our eyes back up above the corners of the table. It's gauche then unifying, so crucial someone tried.

We talk and drink until I'm marshalled (lovingly) home, in case this ship springs a leak too big for the mission and the captain gets all nihilistic.

For these last few days of searching, I have been staying in a sea-facing Leith hotel. The neutrality of the space is reassuring – unsentimental, functional. Despite this lucidity, sleep comes only in teasing chapters, feeling indulgent and futile.

· · ·

You can't be dead because we're still on holiday. Because my brain is still processing the images of the last few days from short-term to long-term memories, and I've not yet shown anyone the pictures from our trip. I've not yet shown anyone the pictures from our trip because I am not yet home from our trip – so you can't be dead. The ink is still wet on the page so there's no way the book's gone up in flames. You can't be dead because we are still mid-conversation on a hundred relatively inconsequential things, and we're about to pick these conversations back up and finish the suckers off like we said we would. Because your litter is in the back of the car and the payment is still processing for the Argyll Smoked Mussels from House of Bruar. Because the moon is the same shape as the moon we feasted under and there's rainwater in my hair from that sudden downpour that caught us out; and I've not yet emptied the sand out my shoes, and I'm still full of the adrenaline from all the fun we had (no, are having!), and my face hasn't stopped throbbing from the laughter clouds we created; and there's that daft sauce stain on my jeans yet to be washed out. You can't be dead because I just got an email about our arrival time from Ullapool Book Festival, and I know the answer to this question, and I don't want to let them down.

. . .

When we parted at Mallarn, I was going to see you again at Ullapool Book Festival – circa 120 hours later. The hours pass, the day arrives. We never made it to Ullapool and yet my mind drifts there incessantly, playing out imagined versions of our capers.

In Ullapool, I knew where we would have stayed and our schedule. I had considered what I would wear, versed out jokes from the recent road trip to contextualise the show. We had discussed food options, nearby walks, the drive to Durness and a Skye-shaped escape the day after – to a place called The Oyster Shed, where a fella called Paul shucks tens of thousands of oysters every year, harvested from his own farm on a nearby loch.

I'm not sure I'll venture back without you. There will be many more events I'll have to sculpt detail around in your absence – Lilongwe, Tokyo, Shetland, New York and sundry others either scheduled or with some planning in place – but none so close to being as Ullapool.

I book another night in the Leith hotel. Hollie handed the plonk from the room back to the reception and asked them not to refill the fridges. As a result, I get shifty looks when dealing with the staff, so make a point of being flamboyantly polite to counteract their suspicions.

Hotels are ports in storms full of people loaded up with memories. So many strangers in these places for the strangest of reasons. I think about what's in between their walls, the bricks and sawdust that buttress the boxes around us. How much of us is hidden in secret spaces, concealed in passageways, or down in the damp cellar? This question requires no resolution, but does serve me notice that it's high time to check out.

But I'm cantankerous at that. Being back in Glasgow is the next chapter of acceptance and I'm still uneasy with its predecessor. The city is haunted, never mind its ghosts.

. . .

When people leave it is commonplace to get together and drink to them; for many centuries this has happened. Rooms filled with kindred communities chortle through batches of tears, embrace rumpus and shatter the awkwardness. The *slàinte* and the silence either pull us together or push us apart.

The first scheduled drinks for you happens above a pub in the west end of Glasgow just minutes from my flat. There is no sandwich spread, though the sunlight is just splendid – big chunky beams shattered to tinsel and splayed across the tables like electric snakes. I invite a couple of people I think you would have wanted there – whose calls I've not taken though I'd love to see them – then worry that I've overstepped the mark by doing so. I recognise fewer of the kind faces than I expect to and that makes me feel small, though it shouldn't. I want to stand on the bar and tell them all about our trip so they know how happy we were just days back, but don't utter a word of it in case that's seen as threatening behaviour. I drink cider to taste like you, and then leave promptly as the room approaches its busiest.

It is often not until such occasions that we realise how self-contained the friendships we had with some people were. How beyond the pale of their wider life, and how deliberately they were kept so. There will always be gangs we are not in. This is how it was before the heartbreak. I remind myself of that and think hard on how many people must be grieving in isolation.

Afterwards, I stay in the Glasgow flat on my own and unpack the bag I've had with me since our trip's fruition. Sand slicks out my shoes. Night unpacks itself and blackens boots; the wind is howling somewhere further north. It is a restless evening and things get drastic in my mind – everyday static becomes shrieking crickets, then yowling cats. I struggle to control the exploding synapses and make the decision that being alone is not the most sensible idea right now.

Immediately I feel myself fighting against the tide of being here. I resolve to leave.

· · ·

Defying all science, grief feels its hottest when newly lit, before it's even started smoking. Before the birds know to stop singing and be forever silent. Before the embargo on mooting a date for the funeral's been lifted. Before one of my friends knows not to throw a strop because I haven't got back to his invite for a camping trip that needs the numbers. Before any notion of talking in the past tense is fathomable. Before Auden's poem 'Stop All the Clocks' could possibly be about you.

It feels like a drug that's newly entered the body and will deliberately dawdle in making the rounds. Inside like a virus. The flesh bullying itself. My vital organs like two best friends who've, for no real reason, fallen out, and on account of their hubris will never find a way back. Grief dissects us into our most helpless matter.

My bones carry an unnatural weight in them, as if the marrow is turning to lead. My gait too is off, like that bike with its bent wheel that required me to cycle like fuck just to make it to the market less than two miles away.

I am on the cusp of crying ordering a cappuccino but ask for chocolate sprinkles all the same, because that's what I used to do, although I've no idea why because I've never had a sweet tooth.

I am desperate for touch, then offended by the suggestion.

I find myself looking into my own eyes in every mirror I pass. Eyes which have become bells that will not stop ringing until the jar cracks or the tongue falls out – either way, it'll be over.

It's being clumsy with meaning, after having prided myself on exactitude, where 140 characters seems a stretch. It feels like I've had my last useful thought and am now salvaging ideas from the mulch.

Time is standing still, until it races by like a cat with a bird in its belly.

Mostly I feel exhausted, slow and eddying, heavier whilst emptied of something I know will never be replenished, that I will always resent living without. I am heartbroken and coarse, whilst acutely thankful for all the wonderful people around me.

I feel important, and guilty about it.

· · ·

Hollie has been checking in on me constantly – keeping vigil, leaving handwritten notes in canny places, running baths when I wouldn't think to, handling the calls I'm not answering. She has been a carer and a confidant, has cancelled work and stalled life. She has provided nurture, consideration, sapience and love. Not only that, but she's also grieving; she abruptly lost a new friend – a loss which she has witnessed crack through the happiness of those close to her. The humans around me are astounding.

I insist she keeps her forthcoming booking at Barcelona International Poetry Festival. I know she wants to. I think she'll be relieved to be in a city of strangers and itinerants, to have a role outside of care-giver. I will join her in Barcelona – I love that city. Yes, a glorious opportunity for fresh oxygen.

· · ·

Aye money has ruined it. For sure, it's been colonised
by cosmopolitan fuckers high on solvency and low on
personality, their mirthless laughter from the bars and cafes
echoing down its narrow streets. But for all those caveats, the
simple fact remains intact: if you don't like Barcelona, you're
a cunt, and totally lost to humanity.

    Irvine Welsh, *Dead Men's Trousers*

I watch the world from a towel-sized balcony twenty storeys up, smear my tongue in the city's salt and listen.

I take off my socks and get sand in between my toes, tunnel down my feet – everything below the ankle in a hot clench. I think of you – just your face as it comes – when my skin tautens plunging into the ocean. You live in my courage now; now and always. I am sorry I couldn't give you more of mine.

Hollie's gig is extraordinary – over a thousand people in a plush concert hall – I am ensorcelled, a thrill I've been missing. It has absolutely nothing to do with your death and so, for a moment, I am out the cage and forgetting to ache.

We meet a Northern Irish friend who's exiled himself from the UK – let's just call it a new beginning. He's loquacious as they come, operating at a hundred miles an hour, hurtling plosives. He mentions you in rapid passing – 'sorry about that' – and then launches into a diatribe about the corporate spunk rats rinsing the city of its edge. It's a startlingly evanescent process, him dealing with this crippling loss before moving onto another tirade. But seeing as the chances of homing my comrade in on a slow elegiac natter are absolutely fucking zilch, the beat comes guilt-free. In this is a softening of my expectations of grief's rigid servitude – that's to say, sometimes it's okay to forcefully forget.

. . .

I head back to Glasgow as AE is arriving from California – I've longed to speak to her in real life, having engaged in a process of passing on our fondest wishes via your texts and tongue. Because of AE's literary ardour you had labelled us friends that should certainly meet. We never quite managed it, so are part-formed things in our requisite minds – yet to exhibit the full canopy of colours. Meeting AE is completing a circle you began drawing.

Before we meet, AE sends me a poem about a magpie and a selkie. I pretend not to have read it, finding it difficult to comment on such things as poetry and the maimed hearts of lovelies.

What I should have said is thank you. It's a fine poem and I'm richer for its coddling of words.

What I should have said is that selkies remind me of Bréon and his mythical Celtic fishing village where music – shot like light into the fouling sea – offers a rope home.

What I should have said is that as a boy I was asked to climb a tree and pierce four magpie eggs with a knitting needle as they lay snug in their nest. This was to prevent another generation of magpies slaughtering the local sparrow, thrush, blackbird and robin population. An act decreed righteous by the adults, the lesser of two evils. An act I agreed to but couldn't perform.

And not for fear of the swooping magpies – for I'd been given a bicycle helmet and goggles – but for fear of the killing, even if they were killers.

What I should have said is that the bird-beak-on-human-face analogy made me recall verse by Katharine Kilalea which opens: 'You were a bird before we met. I know that / because over your skew front teeth / your mouth makes a pointy beak.'

What I should have said is that these (magpies, selkies, Bréon and Katharine Kilalea) are examples of remarkable life-forms, and that this poem has done a great thing in melding them together.

As AE and I spot each other we flail out huge smiles, only later letting ourselves tread into more truthful territory. It reminds me that human countenances are cryptic crosswords and not to be taken lightly. I've friends whom I know to be happy behind the eyes but shite at smiling, armed with faces that just don't give very much – a well-hidden friendly. The opposite can be true too, pain can keep people joking and laughing. Humour is the ideal camouflage for anxiety. I keep this to mind.

Most importantly, I think myself and AE will be friends for years to come. Thank you for the introduction.

. . .

I have a poem in *Oyster* which ends: 'Missing you is not agonising / or forlorn but like being told to turn / down great music you / were about to turn up'.

This was about my adoring and roisterous friendship with Rowley that faded off into the ether. At the moment, missing you is both agonising and forlorn; I would like to make that known. In retrospect, the poem is a misconstruction and not about missing someone at all but about learning to stomach regret.

Losing you is affecting my dreams. Recurring nightmares are no doubt an orthodox part of the grieving process but no less merciless when they arrive.

The recurring nightmare is a clichéd falling scenario. But then again, cliché suggests something that is piffling or benign. I don't think dreams that put you through the wringer can be clichéd, especially when accompanied by sudden jerks and fast blood. I remind myself, with a few tweaks a nightmare is just a dream with a scary scene, and so set about a redraft in the hope of screenwriting my way out of the next one. This is what I used to do with old horror films that frightened me – recast the fear.

Ten fond falls (to bring a little balance):
1. the way apples fall from trees;
2. the way conkers fall from trees;
3. the way pinecones fall from trees;
4. the way coconuts fall from tress (that don't collide with heads). I would like to list lemons, figs, pomegranates and peaches, but will stop here in terms of fruit, nuts and seeds falling from trees;
5. the way rain falls differently on every village, city, town and hat;
6. the way lunar light falls like milk over the moon's rimmed saucer, disrupting even the deepest of dark;

7. the way hair falls by bungee jump, out from a bun or top knot, renewing the face, revisiting a mask;
8. the way mouths fall open when unexpected good news breaks free (especially in hospitals);
9. the way weight falls off when healthy and active – slower and more reasoned than the weight loss of worry;
10. the way eyes fall shut after sunup and sundown safaris, glowing *sui generis* from supreme glimpses into the animal kingdom.

A horny teenage me would have presumed that my first and only recurring dream would be a gumbo of Dionysian pleasure involving paramours and friends and 'the finest wines available to humanity'. I didn't expect my first recurring dream to be of loss with a bark that could shake me awake.

Ten fond things missed more than you:
1. None
2. None
3. None
4. None
5. None
6. None
7. None
8. None
9. None
10. None at all (not even close).

. . .

There is a Neu! Reekie! event in Leith I must present. Two events were previously cancelled for necessity of searching. We have poets over from Georgia and a tenacious Glasgow supergroup primed and ready. Any more cancellations and Neu! Reekie!'s future will be the talk of the town (or so I'm thinking).

There is no pin-badge for grieving a friend, and even if there was I wouldn't wear it despite wanting to. I will instead take the microphone and speak to an audience for the first time since you left. Perhaps over-effervescent or notably lacklustre, it's hard to tell. In this church the acoustics are glorious, the songs and poems are a new cut of worship, the audience in congregation awaits. I tell them a story about you and me in South Africa, a story of four dozing lions and a bull elephant.

———

In Pilanesberg Park we took dusk and dawn runs with naps and swimming in between. We saw warring warthogs, myriad wildebeest and impala, a generous batch of hippos, lions, giraffes, cheetahs, elephants, zebras, rhinos, an African wild dog – the list gusts on. To our amusement, many of the beasts were randy.

Our safari posse included a gaggle of Argentinians who were big *Outlander* fans – though crestfallen to hear we weren't in the show, Caledonia remains next on their holiday bucket list. Our park ranger's name escapes me and I can't text you to ask again, which is a real cunt of a thing. Anyhow, there was this unwritten code that safari goers abide by, a sacred oath of sorts – this being to immediately (I mean IMMEDIATELY) notify the group of significant animal spots. This way the jeep could be swung around and all could behold nature's majesty, democratically, in unison.

Lions, elephants and cheetahs were the paragon sightings and a day had drifted by since any of these beauties surfaced. The light was near done and so our jeep purred off back towards Shepherd's Tree Lodge – eventful enough but all eyes remained thirsty for more.

In this instance, the sky attached its gaze to us, something in the shifting shadows said so. It was just then you tapped me on the shoulder, gestured silently up a steep gradient to a grassy plateau, where a pair of lionesses lay with a pair of cubs sprawled out in a circle, lolling in the sun.

We marvelled a moment, marvelled all over them, took them in with supreme sight-lines and dream-like stillness. Whilst the Argentinians nattered on, garrulous and boozy from a well-oiled rest break, we basked in the company of lions.

A minute or two of spirited silence carried us down the road, until you tapped me once again and mouthed slowly and without a hint of irony, 'Fuck 'em. That was just for us.' And so it was, is and forever will be.

Now I know there's something missing here – the bull elephant. But I'm sorry, that's just for us as well. Maybe one day when the sky is the same mix of thunder, trout and fossil grey, on the brink of musth, will I let it slip, but for now, it remains where it belongs, in the stardust of memory.

What I will say is that at the end of this trip you said to me: 'Well, we know one thing now, Michael. We're fantastic at a holiday. Let's do another.' We toasted to that. I toast to it still.

After the Neu!, a guild of us (Ziggy, Dr Auld, AE, JB and my sister) retire to a one-bedroom apartment in Abbeyhill. This speaks more civilly than perhaps it should; my sister and JB were thoroughly hammered and so AE and I set about making a behemoth pot of pasta to soak up the boozy spills.

Ziggy reveals a hip flask of the rare McClaggan thirty-seven-year-old whisky. This time I take a taste of it and think of your mouth with these flavours lathered all over them. It is easy to do because you had very distinctive lips puffing out beyond a bushy shrubbery of beard. Lips like two tracks well trod, flourishing, full and ripe. I sip with them in mind.

Ziggy tells me he still has your empty cider bottles in the kitchen of The Lengths in Achaflute; loose change by the bed you slept in has not been removed – a wee pile of coins pyramiding up. These are nothing really, overspill, the left-behind, but on them are fingerprints, saliva, tracks of life. The chance for a memory to erupt out of them – a desultory sentiment to some, a worthy tribute to others.

The night ends in a bed ill-equipped to deal with one hunk of flesh, never mind the three warriors piled into it. Despite the lacking ergonomics, I sleep soundly, in the heat of friends.

· · ·

Sometimes there are places we need to head to compute loss. These could be new spots frequented with purpose or familiar haunts steeped in nostalgia. The Scottish Borders is one such place, a visit best done in a coven.

We stay at The Abbey Hotel, which overlooks the 'remarkably complete' ruins of an old abbey and looms over the River Tweed. To the best of my knowledge, it is the only hotel around these parts with an indoor pool. This area, like much of the Borders, has a turbulent and violent history as disputed terrain. Aesthetically, however, it's stunning – a wreath of heather, forest, river and birdsong. The area is synonymous with the writer Walter Scott and so the name Scott is emblazoned all about – Scott Street, Scott Crescent and, most notably, Scott's View. But truth be told the swimming pool is of most interest to me at the moment, and although you are not here to be coerced into photographing me 'dicking about' in it, I shall horseplay and tomfool like you are.

Before tracking down the pool, Hollie, AE and I find ourselves rock dancing over the fringes of the river. We are answerable only to the light ricocheting, and discuss the sun's showboating – slinging colour around like a drunk painter. Not a second wasted, I'm swimming in the river, not risking missing this, fully clothed or not.

We each squawk when crotch meets gelid stream, yet soon enough we're paddling and baying in rapture. AE is wearing a grandiose floral dress and emerges from the water looking Dickensian as fuck. We are dressed in the river and it is wearing us.

A romp of ducks gawp on incredulous. The keen anglers twenty metres upstream are even less impressed having paid top dollar for their permit to fish 'the remote' crusts of the River Tweed. Enraged, in full regalia, they shoot us eye daggers. I posit this is not how they expected their river privileges to look.

In due course, I notice all the rooms here are named after different types of fishing flies. Mine is Jock Scot, the nom de plume of a punk poet we've been deeply entangled with at camp Neu! Reekie!. He too has recently departed this planet, leaving many decades of wise and unwise words behind him. The room next door has Willie Gunn emblazoned on it. It deals up a photo opportunity you'd not have seen us miss.

Today we were synced in time and place; in our numbers we ganged thigether without you for the first time. Some of us will probably avoid each other afterwards; others will too zealously smoosh up against one another, desperate for touch. I hope there was some fingering and fucking after but I do not know. Perhaps you do and were watching? Dirty bugger.

· · ·

You are the only friend whose death I've rehearsed. Your leaving was within the realms of my imagination; I have visited it (before it was a thing), sat on a bench beside my inner conscience and cogitated how I might weather it.

This is because you sang about leaving this world before and talked openly about how close it had come for you, whilst prosaically acknowledging the speed at which the darkness could return. In the shadows of knowing you well lurked the fear of losing you far too soon. This suggests a more lugubrious you than you – not the you that was you, always so damn inspiring, quick-witted, full of laughter and élan. I know this is the type of you I was allowed to see but it was magnificent and most commonly around. Foremost, I remember you laughing.

. . .

This is the last day of May, which means the first month of you not being alive will soon begin, and the world's chance to rectify its big mistake is about to expire. I make a vow to keep a log of this altered passage through time, in order to help me digest how the weeks function without you.

I expect a bell-ringing ceremony and prophetic gongs. The day, instead, brings me a missed-delivery slip and a low-ink warning from the printer.

I'm trying to stay home for longer, but the room feels more like a prison than a refuge so I head for the parkland. Frisked by wind, I take the uphill, gallop against it until my feet growl. I stare longingly into the eyes of every curious animal that stops to investigate my shadow, hoping for that impossible snap of familiarity – hoping to see a friend reincarnate. I sit on a slanted rock and watch the sun slalom around me until settling on my lap like a warm-bellied dog. I pick this spot, crotch warming, and meditate on the fabulous cocks you've drawn. Amongst other accolades, you were the most talented cock drawer I ever knew.

There is an exquisite member in the gutter of the draft cover you drew for *Oyster*. The draft and the final specimen were exhibited in Johannesburg and purchased by a fan and fine-fettled champion of all things you. He posted this cock online. Alongside it two cocks hidden within his signed copy of the book – a token of authenticity. I was very pleased to see these throbbing members paraded out. The raggedy cumbersome cock atop the Scottish Saltire is mine. The well-defined beaming baton on his page sixty-nine is yours.

These cocks were drawn on our last night of The South African Tour in a moment of exultation. Drawn on a terrace high above Joburg in a hilltop hideaway. In the gloaming the skyline turned out like a Van Gogh: medallions and florals, geometric spinning. We made our mark out there.

You slipped a much subtler phallic sketch onto the front cover of *Oyster*. That and a straight-up expletive – the publisher has not yet spotted these. The game to find these profanities is called 'Spot the Boaby Fuck'. A new town lotto with a stale fruitcake as a prize (that may or may not have been indecently tampered with).

. . .

The most common check-ins come with a command of honesty.

> *Be honest, how are you holding up?*
> *Honestly now! I want to know.*

My heart is buckled by love lost, peeled inside out, all onion gook, a rabbit skinned alive, a tongue slashed in half. I cannot answer this.

Amongst all the untested theories and white noise, it will take longer to be honest, to understand what honest really means here; to know how far to push it.

. . .

I read poems to a group at a house gig; the last one is about you. People cry and laugh and smile and though I have to depart promptly, I do so leaving a litter of folks sharing stories about you and making notes to follow up on. It is the right way to leave a room.

I head off to attend a Young Fathers concert at Leith Theatre. I have grown up in Edinburgh over the same period as Young Fathers. The sermons this band uncage upon crowds are stupendous. To listen to YF live is to be engulfed within a cosmic storm. Their performance is imbued with snippets of adulation for the Leith stalwarts and accounts of what the occasion means to the band. It means a lot to me. Alongside the music, spears of politically charged chants are launched into the euphoric sweating horde.

Being in amongst music like this is something I needed to do. I get rhapsodic, blow a casket, empty and refill. But the lingering snarl of the poem plus the eruption of Young Fathers proves too much too soon and I unravel into a febrile, plangent state.

I get home later than I should with gaping gaps in the night. Wake not in my scratcher but on a friend's shit futon, as close to a bed of nails as it comes. How quickly we crumble. I skinned my knees and my chin took a dunt. Essentially, I made a right cunt of myself, but people are forgiving.

I vow to withdraw for a week or two: tread softly, avoid alcohol. I hide away until it's time to leave the country for a (now ludicrous-sounding) birthday trip. In contemplating the indulgence of this I'm reminded of these lines from *Harry Potter and the Deathly Hallows*.

Ginny Weasley: Seems silly, doesn't it? A wedding. Given everything that's going on.
Harry Potter: Maybe that's the best reason to have it. Because of everything that's going on.

. . .

It is mid-June and turns my birthday in a charismatic beer bar in Perugia, the capital city of the district of Umbria in Italy. The bar, Elfo, is situated at the bottom of a steep snaking alleyway and has a green light outside to let you know it's safe to enter. In on the green, I'm with close company, devoted faces with warm cores. Myself, Hollie and some friends (Clee and Nicole) drink to health and Italy's culinary domination – there is cherry beer, salted snacks and kissing. Amongst the gaiety, I sneak away and have a wee seat in the toilet, talk to you and cry.

The next morning after a wonderful night loneliness jolts me up. I am full of love, surrounded by friends, sticky, naked, full and yet haunted by absence. I think how irked you'd be by my dull, lingering soupiness, and so set about learning the type of new things I could have dropped into conversation over our dinners. I'm in Italy, for fuck's sake.

I learn of Perugia that it has been a thriving centre of artistic commissions, building and construction, but also the site of a great many Italian wars – namely because of its resistance to papal rule. In the summer of the year 1500, an infamous slaughter took place at a Baglioni family wedding – Perugia's ruling crew, yet a people wrought with infighting and imbroglios. This fateful incident would change the course of history for the region. Essentially, disgruntled members of the Baglioni family used the grand celebration as an opportunity to settle a family feud – a power grab in which, at the wedding celebrations, they slayed nearly two hundred important guests (many of them their own relations). The groom himself (Astorre Baglioni) meeting the most brutal end – his chest cut open and his heart removed, with one of the foremost assailants taking a ceremonial bite out it. This episode, known as 'The Bloody Wedding', triggered a guilt-ridden Atalanta Baglioni to commission a young Raphael to paint a new work in memory of her murdered son. A son to whom she had refused refuge during the fracas, and who was later slain. The work, *The Deposition*, is still on display in Rome. The reason for this aberration into gory Italian history is that this massacre bears a striking resemblance to a famous episode of *Game of Thrones* called 'The Red Wedding' – an episode we discussed in depth. This discovery is exactly the type of hot take that would have lit up a dinner session, something I'm gutted not to be able to share with you. So here it is, just in case.

. . .

After a couple of nights in Perugia, exclusively dedicating our time to the city's culinary trail, we quest off in a hire car into the Umbrian countryside.

Tucked away down an inconspicuous dirt road, we find La Fonte, a farmhouse drowned in eighteen hectares of fields and woods. We dismount the vehicle and are immediately greeted by the air's floral pepper. The welcome party includes dogs, cats, goats, chickens, and the Milanese family who keep the plot.

We cook, chatter and chart the land. I'm asked about how the hurt is going and given ample leeway to steer the conversation into or away from you. Friends consoling friends really is a miraculous thing. It baffles me that some folks simply cease going on holiday with friends when in a romantic coupling, as if this somehow eliminates the need for all other forms of enchantment.

Evening brings a carnival of chirrups, howls, clucks, rustles, hoots, trills, clicks and clacks to soundscape our outdoor dining. No need for music when cadenzas such as these swim the air. I have not felt a peace like this since before you left.

I doze through the morning, finding the sleep I missed out on in May. In the afternoon, I take a long directionless walk to where the grass grows waist-high, knotty and thick, and the light turns to powder. Like hundreds of people who miss you, I am carrying you with me.

On the final day at La Fonte, Hollie and I set off towards some ruins on the highest peak in this chain of mountains. Flash fast, the smell of the soil and the song of the insects are totally unfamiliar. We submit to a complete unawareness of the area – I'd have been no less surprised to have seen our tapir charging out the thick bushes than a coyote or a kangaroo. What I didn't expect to see was a 'Beware American Pit Bull' sign.

We discover the ruins of the chapel we are trekking to have become the camp for a squad of Italian travellers. The sketchy sign is to warn off straying amblers. To exclaim the point, an angry dog face is also drawn on the signage. As much as I want to behold the ruins, as arduous as the slog under the spiking sun is, I'm not risking a pit bull bite. I've seen this breed of canine at its most menacing, a stark reminder of the plight of poor wee Corky back on the M'hudi ranch. I remember telling you this story; your chortling, grin and gasp come flooding back. I shouldn't chuckle. I do.

. . .

Hollie, Clee and Nicole head home and I'm handed over to Bréon.

Bréon and his partner Garry live here in the golden yolk of Umbria. They travel constantly, so capturing them in their home habitat comes with the thrill of a rare wildlife spot.

I am not tinkering with trouble today but intrepidly walking the peaks, slipping with (not against) the soil. The hills here are densely populated by bustling trees and other ramose greenery; long stretching branches that rally the sky. The leaves are palmate, with green fingers pointing back towards Cascaroni. Only when far off, looking through the gossamer gauze of hot air, can you really appreciate its cradle on the mountainside.

Cascaroni is a stunning property and sprawling grounds that spill over several levels and involve a gorgeous mix of gradients; it has its own earthy arithmetic. It is somewhere hearts come to heal.

On one of our many walks, Bréon mentions that he will name his writing cabin after the Shepherd's Tree Lodge and will plant a pomegranate tree for you. In fact, it has already been planted but is experiencing some relocation trauma – once it pulls past winter it will become your tree. Something will be said in the new season for its valour.

Roslyn is my chosen walking stick – much like a wizard chooses their staff. It is stapled to my side for leverage on the steep gradients. In Umbria, the stick is a weapon should we encounter the *cinghiale*. Elsewhere in the world, Roslyn is a feeling against my thigh reminding me to stay strong.

The pool at Cascaroni is the reward – a fence of bamboo shields it, keeping it cool. The sun can only skate around the water's edge chasing the winged insects. It appears as if plucked out of a David Hockney painting. The countdown before jumping into the freezing water plays inside me like a flute.

From the top tier of Cascaroni, we catapult your music across the canopies and flood the valley below. Sound disturbs the speckled butterflies in the overgrown amphitheatre, makes the frogspawn tremble. I've no doubt the music flumes all the way to Montone – Umbria's hilltop Valhalla.

Kindred hits from your oeuvre cut the hour-long walk across the mountain crowns down to the crackle of seconds. Music makes the type of shortcut only those with wings can take. I trust when your words land in Piazza Fortebraccio they knock gelato from the cone of an awestruck citizen.

I play song after song, twinned with story after story, and

Bréon and Garry simply listen. Showing their appreciation for this Etruscan disco, the barking deer deep in the forest's shadowland let loose their inimitable call. Not to be outdone, the fireflies, who've gathered for us, soak the air in gold.

Caught in the canorous splendour of it, Garry suggests a caterpillar crawling along a wine bottle could be a message from the spirit world. The electric green lizard with its stomach splooshed across the hot slab makes more sense to me. The caterpillar is placed back upon the greenery, the lizard scuttles off towards a fig tree, and we continue entertaining notions of an afterlife.

. . .

I am back in Glasgow. You are still gone. It's not yet settled; there are voices in the trees. You disappeared and the sun has not stopped shining – it's no coincidence; the world up high has something to say about this.

Auden in his poem 'In Memory of W. B. Yeats' says: 'he became his admirers'. Although many would jostle for this conclusion, today it feels as if you have become the heat on our skin. Missing you, something leaving from inside of us, has been narrated by a Scottish heatwave.

Today (28/06/18) in Glasgow it was 32°C – Scotland's hottest day in twenty-three years and close to the highest recorded Scottish temperature of 32.2° captured in 1893 in Ochtertyre in Perth and Kinross. Trains were cancelled as tracks became malleable, the electrics went bonkers and road surfaces melted. On a weather map Scotland is a scorched satsuma and I am walking miles risking burnt eyelids to tire myself out.

. . .

I get an oyster tattoo, my first tattoo. I have always deemed my mind too flippant, too prone to caprices, to settle on an image that will chum me through life. This has changed things. Like counting stars, I will not tire of recounting the tale of this oyster inking.

An amazing Edinburgh artist called Sarah Muirhead does the needling for me. She draws spectacularly, has a proclivity for painting the scarred and muscular, contortionists, the fantasticism of flesh. She has morphed her skill of painting the heavily tattooed into tattooing. You, too, enjoyed her work and thus it is ratified that she should be the artist to interpret your oyster illustration on my skin.

This oyster tattoo is the fulfilment of a pact.

———

It started on a hillside above a village hall on Iona in July 2017. You had played music and I had spoken words at Roddy Woomble's Festival – a dreamboat of a trip.

Late that first night, the sky a smear of astral light, we consorted – snuck off to a sequestered spot. Somewhere up in the spacy thick of it a satellite called Cassini was taking pictures of Saturn's rings; we talked about all the great work it had done and the injustice that lay ahead – a 75,000 miles per hour plunge into space debris.

We mapped movements for our impending trips and took stock of things that make hearts sink and swell. Just before we headed back into the clamour you said one last thing: 'We should get matching oyster tattoos after the tour.' I cheerily committed as the wind began to wag its tail across our skin.

Over the remainder of summer and autumn 2017, we did the tour and slurped down many different types of oysters, but the matter of tattoos wasn't raised again until our last dinner together in Mallarn in May 2018 (our last dinner together being one of your last suppers full stop). As you'll recall, we were talking about your illustrations and, as these things often do, this led to tattoos. The meal ended, post platter and post pudding, with you reminding me of those matching oyster inkings we'd made a covenant to get. 'I'm still up for it,' you said. 'I've not forgotten.'

———

Post Mallarn, I do not see you again, so you do not have yours. But Mallarn is the last night I spend with you and so I have mine. Perhaps it was just a quicksilver remark, maybe it was something more; either way I've taken it to oath – inked it on me, then again.

I wanted this tattoo before heading off to The Curfew Tower. But just moments before so as not to have to explain it to anyone the Scotland side of the Irish Sea.

The ink has dried below my skin, its pigment underneath my dermis the most permanent aesthetic decision I've taken. I'm pleased to welcome it aboard my body. I think of it: there's a sadness in some happiness that can sink a ship, but only if you let it. In essence, the ink is a form of praise. On Keats's grave-stone in Rome it is etched: 'Here lies One Whose Name was writ in Water'. A self-deprecating epitaph later regretted by the friends who chose it, but there's no denying the slip of beauty it conjures. For in our language, you are now writ on me.

4

The Tackle Shop Eternal

Fright, the swine, yanks me out a dream – a sharper awakening than a wet dream but better than a pissy pants incident at a sleepover. Hands pleached, I wake as if I went to sleep with a bird in the oven.

In my dream I sat on a verdant hillside and studied a cityscape in heightened detail – all rococo in its brushstrokes – the light bending purple from a sassy tangerine. It was Edinburgh, yes, but ten times its usual size. On my favourite street I unfankled like an old man napping on a park bench.

You were there too, living in this city, alongside many versions of me. I would lose you then find you again, as happens at festivals. All good fun until a malaise moved in as a sea haar might. And then a crack in the ether revealed the sky had been a glass dome all along. Shards like tusks raining down. We found cover under a bus shelter and from our point of safety pledged to repair the humongous snow globe unbuckling above us, knowing fine well it simply couldn't be done.

Out the dream, I remind myself to always bask in the freshness in waking, celebrating life on behalf of those who've lost it. You are five months gone and, though the shock has ebbed, the hurdles ahead produce a riptide of anxiety.

I reconfigure, ponder the fabular story my mind just cooked up whilst brewing coffee and dancing naked to your music.

I reassure myself that what is best remembered are the words people left us with when most themselves, not those put in their mouths by the grieving: me, us, others.

I have seen hundreds of poets, singers, actors and artists perform – from commercial successes to cult heroes, the avant-garde to the outrageous, stadium fillers to online superstars. There are few that could match your iridescence. I thought that before I loved you. Now that I do, now that you're lost, I feel it rising everywhere.

There were so many fantabulous fragments of you to frolic with; too much beautiful human for just one man. Everyone is missing you differently, pining for separate pieces, incomplete in incomparable ways.

Your songs are outpourings, confessionals, tender hymns of understanding – the human soul deep in despair. There are so many avenues into your emotions in these words that thousands find themselves feeling more complete within them. At the core of it all is a quest for love and happiness – you augment and pass on lessons learned, hoping for more inspired results amongst us listeners.

You have bequeathed to us an armour, gifted us a gallantry you weren't able to fully utilise – for many this is the will to keep moving. Your fragility sprang up and out from inside, there really was no other way for you. Your friendship was the catalyst I needed to become my braver self, to ameliorate. This is not a gift given only to me (far from it) but to an enormous family of us the world over. What a priceless memory. What colossal connection.

After a successful press launch for a play about a poet Bréon's bringing to Scotland, I leave Edinburgh by train, spat out at the Glasgow end weary and unsteadied. Early October chill invisibled by booze. I fear bumping into people in such a state and this time the fear is realised. I crash into a friend of yours amidst the hubbub of Sauchiehall Street on a Friday night – this being Glasgow's main drag of fast food, dark drinks, blood and debauchery; quite the spectacle and highly recommended.

I pluck off his ear and lament gloop down it, inject clunky words into it. Here is a face who misses your face whom I have not seen since you left. Raddled and pulverised, this sparks the fiery notion that it's a ripe time to talk. His ear listens, I have stolen it – a mendicant. It absorbs, sympathises and I return it to his face (mostly unharmed). Stitching it back on, if you must know.

He – now two-eared again – shares in the story, lets me know how much he too misses you, and then concludes by noting the recent passing of two of his immediate family. This gentle comment is a metal rod up the arse of a numpty (*moi*) without a lick of grease. I feel heavy for having cadged the airwaves and pilfered his ear. I make my excuses and leave like a dope in gloryless guilt.

I must be careful how I talk to people in moments of emotional extremity. Despite my own emergencies, I have no idea the size of the mountains of shit people may have just climbed out of. I must go home and think about these matters at once.

. . .

Come the end of October I venture out to a live show once again. I'm tiptoeing back into it after the last gig meltdown. I'm trepidatious, sure, but it's one of the places I feel most alive, certainly most distracted. The two sentiments, at the moment, share a spinal cord. Besides, the show is Hollie, so I can't miss it.

This is gig number three for Hollie at Glasgow's Òran Mór but the dynamics of the room have shoogled about since my last visit. There's a rasp in the air, in my ears at least. The seats in front are where you, Mally and I sat last year at Hollie's show. Whether consciously or not, I'm back in the exact same position in the room.

Sure, places have memories of us the way we have memories of them. Often, I picture rooms we've been in with us back in them. I'm inexorably hounding the spectres of our past selves. Tonight, I have found them here in frocks and fandango. Back in that moment we are all ghosts of the same tribe. Site-specific memories are my favourite form of time travel.

During the performance, something quite unthinkable happens: your face appears in the disco ball that hovers above the audience. Smirking face in a disco ball lightning in my chest. This is my Allen Ginsberg-meets-William Blake moment – a touching of the void, a purpose-plump visitation beyond anything to date. I mean, you ken I'd have been here if you'd seen the listings. Would hang here now and again catching all the shows for free, right at the front but not blocking anyone's view on account of being another form of matter.

A likely hallucination, but what a pleasing way to receive

signals from beyond – a smile and a shadowy beard network laced over shimmering silver panels. It lasted around a minute, passed faster than a flush and, at the same time, kept something of me.

I hope it was you in that mirror-ball matrix and please come back soon. And even if it wasn't, I felt something and cherish it still. It was the whisk and whisper in the rhythm of life. I am a disco casualty yearning for more Donna Summer.

Stop by any time, chances are I'll be thinking about you:
1. any time I'm scared;
2. any time I'm angry;
3. any time I'm empty;
4. any time I'm rushing towards something I shouldn't be;
5. any time confronted by the verisimilitudes of ocean;
6. any time analysing graphs on my Sleep Cycle app seeking the chance to compare data;
7. any time in Glasgow – I live in Glasgow;
8. any time in a swimming pool 'dicking about';
9. any time there are new tattoos;
10. any time there's beard to scrunch;
11. any time drinking more than I ought to;
12. any time sad the morning after;
13. any time when in or moving between Cushendall and Cape Town; The Curfew Tower and The Grey Hotel;
14. any time carrying a guitar to share the load;
15. any time watching *Game of Thrones* or during the post-episode evaluation;

16. any time there are flowers by a roadside (such ghastly beauty);
17. any time I forget the details of a story only you can finish;
18. any time giggling;
19. any time on my future thirty-seventh birthday;
20. any time Tom Petty lopes onto a speaker system;
21. any time with smoked mussels / every form of messy seafood. After all, oysters are best when part of a smorgasbord;
22. any time upset by people's mean remarks;
23. any time M'hudi lipped;
24. any time a song lyric rises up inside me;
25. any time I dream or nightmare, which come so close together now;
26. any time an owl hoots to celebrate the evasion of an awkward encounter;
27. any time the phone rings, then stops;
28. at Christmas;
29. any time someone suggests a visit to a zoo in place of a safari;
30. any time someone compliments or chides my book, which is also your book;
31. any time stalking cats holding back their purr;
32. sometimes when I'm snogging – is that a little (Winifer) Odd?;
33. any time;
34. all the time;

35. I need time;

36. & you.

. . .

I have gone many places contemplating your passing, bundled my bones into neutral spaces, kept my mind running and the scenery flowing. I have been as purposely out of Glasgow's arms as any hugger can be.

Now, something new, Bag End (or rather a miniature replica hobbit house outside of Dunblane). Though bereft of electricity, the cosy abode was fitted with gas hobs, wood fire, solar-powered lanterns, compost toilet, candles, a hobbit-sized bath, a white Highland koo, owls on the bedposts, and a skylight framing the interstellar. They've gone the extra mile to create a Middle Earth transformation, not a cheap stay but sedulously crafted, family-run and worth every penny when tackling love lost.

With that said, I ken my grief has been privileged. It is privilege that I can let it distil and analyse it, physically and emotionally; that I can take time away from everyone and immerse myself in countryside or busy crowds; that I can travel to see friends and go off-grid.

Grief can be expensive and yet instinctively feels it should be unshackled from money or economies of scale. It should undoubtedly be tax deductible. As with most things, wealth makes elements of grieving more amenable. That said, I'm fresh out of a fucking tower and into a fantasy 'hole in the ground' whilst chatting about international travel, and I have a shite annual income, so I'm not offering much credence to that theorem. I do, however, benefit from being able to take off unannounced without answering to anyone or any assets. This might suggest my privilege is also a form of loneliness.

My first night in Bag End (aka Craighead Howf) and I end up crying. But on this occasion the tears are cathartic, thankful sobs in honour of the one-year anniversary of our time in South Africa.

If little fragments of us end up all over the world, anchors of light beaded into the air, then a part of you is in South Africa. A part of me too. I trust they're together, up to all sorts, scheming a jamboree.

I ardently message my old pen-friend from the unofficial Tolkien fan club about these digs. He is watering tomatoes and listening to an unabridged audio book version of *The Fellowship of The Ring* when the message comes through. Shire-sized synergy that – no fucking kidding, my darling boy all but injects Tolkien into his bloodstream!

His, out of orbit, friendship has permeated high school to present day. A bond preceded by a botched attempt to secure a pen-friend from the back of a football magazine called *Shoot*. The premise was to link up with a fan of a football club from a different part of the UK and share scores and musings on the sport. Several months in, my pen-friend called an end to the correspondence. He stated that although I was a keen writer, I scarcely mentioned football and didn't seem in any way curious about his team. My sporting analogies had waned, petered out, at times completely absent. This curt dismissal, although upsetting, was fair. I was looking for something of deeper feeling.

Several years later, I garrisoned the gumption to re-enter the pen-friend game. This time post a real-life encounter on a family coach holiday. His name was also Michael, he hailed from Berkshire and was a Tolkien enthusiast. Michael kept me up to date with all the goings-on in the Tolkien fan club and, later, would make me mix-tapes of sagacious sixties and seventies songwriters. He came to visit me in Edinburgh years later, at eighteen, having never kissed anyone and left having kissed someone. It was not me, but I like to think I nourished the smooch. I found a fit with Michael and we're friends still.

The last time I saw him was at our *Oyster* launch in London at The Social. Everyone that was important to me I wanted you to meet, by seeing them you saw a little more of me.

Despite this heart-warming exchange with Michael, and the memories it whips up, I soon find myself keening. Struck by the notion that perhaps it was a mistake to come to Bag End. That perhaps this writing is too big for me, too risky. In order to pacify crashing thoughts, I park my tribulations and take to walking. Out to the hillside to converse with the Shetland ponies and dwarf goats that complete this fantasy. Hands mummified in their pocket tombs, a Baltic wind slaps my wrists.

And then it comes to me. Fucking Tolkien! He was born in South Africa. Like M'hudi's snog and Katharine Kilalea and that fact that the whole time I'm here the ghosts of us are there this time last year! And Bill Drummond, my now friend / the owner of Curfew, he's South African born too.

I can't resist investigating how much of South Africa made it into *The Lord of the Rings*. Research leads me to believe Tolkien left very young, his most vivid memory: being bitten by a baboon spider. I realise what's more important is that the boldest love alive in *The Lord of the Rings* is the friendship between Frodo and Sam. It is Frodo's best friend Sam that will continue his story in The Shire; it is Sam he kisses last before sailing to the Undying Land of the Elves. Some say he will join him there.

Okay, perhaps coming to Bag End has purpose beyond my cognisance; perhaps it's showing me the way. A story about you comes back as if summoned.

———

We got to Joburg airport jauntily early, ready for the short flight to Cape Town. Guitar and luggage checked in and through security with the slippery ease of a flume ride. You were a nervous flyer, the short-haul ones the worst, smaller planes more susceptible to sweeping winds. Your short-haul psyche less accepting of the journey ahead on account of the high ratio of upheaval to small amount of time travelled. The seats tended to be filled with more agitated work flyers. The flights offer fewer free drinks, snacks and sources of entertainment to placate bellicose temperaments. At least that was the way of things on budget airline FlySafair, which claims to be home of the Springboks (South Africa's national rugby team).

To help fluff up your courage, a couple of Long Island iced teas and a bowl of nibbles were deemed necessary before the aeronautic ordeal. The thing is, the airport was busy, the cocktails well crafted, and our flight was inexplicably (and unbeknown to us) moved from 18.00 to 17.55. Long story short, by the time we'd crunched through the last of the ice in our glasses, and joined the wrong queue, we'd missed the flight and our luggage had been hoofed off the plane.

The air stewardesses, with whom we'd had a bit of a giggle upon check-in, began mock applauding when we came back hangdog to collect our haul. Quickly turning more earnest, they enquired as to what happened and expressed concern for the gig we had to play later that night. The show was actually a few days off but still needed playing and the seriousness of us not making it to Cape Town was heightened by their confusion.

We were entered in the seat lottery for no-shows on the fully booked 20.00 flight, the last of the night. We bumbled back an hour later along with a pen of hopefuls wearing our best crestfallen faces. The matriarch readied herself for the roll call, soon to be naming four of twelve who would be journeying forth. I felt like a hopeful actor trying to stick out from the crowd at the gate of a Hollywood studio – face jutting forwards against the iron bars that held back my dreams. A small wink from the second steward in command alluded to our numbers coming in. And so they did. And so we fist-pumped the air, embraced, and let our loads lighten.

That said, it wasn't a sure thing just yet; the mission still involved a lissome sprint to the gate, which was now blinking final call. We redeposited our belongings and summoned the chutzpah of the cheetah brothers we'd seen prowling the grounds of Pilanesberg.

The flight hit the troposphere at 20.10 with our warm bums buckled in tight. You zoned into a podcast and we smirked through the whole journey. A better prescription for air-travel anxiety than any notion we could have invoked a couple of hours back.

Although we made it to Cape Town, my luggage and your guitar did not. We were assured the last-minute dash of our load-on had simply left the baggage handlers unable to catch the aircraft before the hold was locked. Assured that our gear would be on the next flight over and couriered directly to our hotel. No worries, we were feeling lucky to be here, left the details of our lodgings and sprung off gaily.

Our belongings didn't arrive that night, but we weren't overly concerned. The trouble was, we were still bereft of our possessions two days later – despite being told they would be on the morning flight, then the afternoon service, and then the evening call. But nope, nothing, zilch, diddly-squat, each enquiry met with a newfangled excuse for their non-appearance. A tincture of the wild goose chase started to seep in, and the show approached – you instrumentless more of a pickle than me without my polka dot pants.

We solved the more immediate dilemma. I bought new clothes from a nearby mall and you borrowed a guitar from a Malawian troubadour (George Kalukusha) who was teaming in on the show. I arrived clean and comfortable and you sang as if made of butter and peppercorns.

On our penultimate day in Cape Town, FlySafair came clean on something they'd been glossing over. They in fact didn't know where our stuff was. Our items were registered as having been loaded onto the same flight we boarded in Johannesburg but never bleeped in at Cape Town. They announced with a cackle: it's so bizarre, as if the stuff just disappeared mid-air. They were, however, obstreperous in their resolve not to close the case or offer compensation as the team continued the search.

You took to social media and had a fun and feisty gripe about the position they'd left us in – having to badger them for answers. Cue a pile-on from justice-seeking fans of your music with a few threatening to boycott the airline if there wasn't a satisfactory resolution. This upped the ante of their search and on our last day in Cape Town we received a call to say the luggage had finally been found. In Gaborone, Botswana.

We were told, however, not to fret as someone was already driving the cargo down from Botswana and would be meeting us back in Johannesburg to oversee, and photograph, our grand reunion. The latter to appease any rankled onlookers following the saga.

Later that night, a veil of silliness stuck to our skins as we waited to board the budget airline. Carriers of the Springboks, eh, hope they don't fly on a match day, the strips might end up in Lagos. But let's get real, when have the national rugby team ever flown FlySafair? And then, in some form of divine jibbing, a huddle of the Springboks shuffled straight past us in team tracksuits. They wound their way to the front of the queue taking courteous selfies and having genial exchanges along the way. Well, fuck a duck, there they are. Wouldn't have thought they'd even fit in one of these metal birds. And they barely did.

The chatter on the journey was lilted, the flight attendants blushed and the captain gave a chipper call-out. Our faces bloomed brighter for the mountainous men's presence. The tiny reading lamps became spotlights on their flesh. We all stole concupiscent glances. Caged in, their muscular thighs pushed away from their genitals like giant barbecue tongs released from the restraints. Their shoulders like the humps on camels, whilst glistening pretty as iced buns. Humans as strong and taut as they were in their singularity can look out of place with the world around them. En bloc, armed as we were with the knowledge of their sporting pedigree, they were astonishing, like a fleet of beautiful boats. Bizarre to think the vast majority of these powerful beings were considerably younger than us, newer to the news.

I mooted at what age they had become too big to climb trees but then remembered the giant redwoods I'd seen in California that could grow to over 250 feet tall, and over twenty-five feet in diameter, living for thousands of years. A passenger informed me that South Africa's biggest tree, the Sagole Baobab, could likely host them all for a picnic in its nest-like branches.

I bet their mums never heckled them, calling them 'a big bitch' at their own gig. This didn't happen to me but to my friend Dominic, yet we all laughed nervously about it because it could have been any of us – a mum, auntie or cousin turned corrupt with the power of a platform.

You pointed out that this was a safe flight, that this plane would not be going down, not with the Springboks on it, not on home soil.

The atmosphere was that of sitting in a hot spring by a stream of meltwater – aroused by our collective talking point; a general moistening. People wanted to touch them; some did. The conversations that resulted were tenebrous. With a complete stranger we began discussing voyeurism. Had the players begun wanking each other off it would have been treated with cheer, likely deemed a show of national pride or a pre-match superstition to be encouraged. We accepted we'd have been swept up in the jubilation, applauding effusively for their splendid carnival of penis – cocks lined up like the spine of a Stegosaurus.

Upon landing, everyone clapped and whooped: for the touchdown, for the players, for the magic in the air. We felt stronger for having shared Springbok vapour, co-habited this metal village in the sky.

Plodding down the airstairs, we noticed a swanky Mercedes stretch splitter van parked beside the plane for the Boks. In front of it two young women in chintzy cheerleader uniforms waved a welcome banner. We wanted a look in that vehicle – music blaring, it was like something from a badly shot hip-hop video.

As we hit concrete the heat pressed down from above and bounced up from below, but the conglomerate shadow of the rugby titans offered us sweet relief. Being this close also meant getting a neb into their deluxe wagon without appearing blatant. We kept tight to them as the first couple of players beelined towards the opened doors of the Mercedes. But something unusual happened: the young attendant, clearly star-struck, remorsefully turned away the national heroes. The great men had no option but to thump off towards the cattle bus ready for its drive to the terminal. The laminated sign the young women were brandishing, in fact, had our names on it. It seemed, after the social media traction, FlySafair were going the extra mile to ensure we were blissfully reunited with our belongings – namely you and your guitar, but my pants were along for the ride.

Surprised as anyone, we stottered onto the leather seats, accepted glasses of iced water and cold face towels. Our eyes, through the open doors of the splitter, met those of the players wedged onto the bus. They were curious as to who had the gravitas to usurp the national team from their leather thrones. We stared back mortified, as if to say we'd give up these bum cushions in a heartbeat if we could – we wanted them to know they'd rainbow-stamped our day. They laughed, we laughed and the moment split open like a juicy orange, leaving everyone revitalised and sticky.

'That the fricking Springboks you guys were travelling with?' the driver shouted, volleying his winsome voice off the rear-view mirror.

'Oh yeah,' I said, 'we go ways back. Now howz about that grand homecoming with my undergarments? I'm onto the second day with this pair and there's dancing to be done.'

———

Lots of couples have left loving remarks in the Bag End guest-book with quotes from Tolkien and hints at the amorous benefits of hobbit role play in this remarkable location. I, too, leave a scribble to mark my time here but, unlike all the hobbit shaggers, have produced no love paste.

So as to play ball, I will masturbate tonight pretending to be a hobbit reflecting on a romantic encounter at the Green Dragon and will try not to let your lovely big face come cameo-ing in at the crucial moment. If it does, I won't let it stop me. Not exactly an erudite ending to this entry but it'll have to do. Besides, I'm pretty sure a hobbit wank would have you laughing more than any profundities I couldn't think of.

. . .

You have a bench in Glasgow's Kelvingrove Park, mere minutes from my flat. It's a couple of months old by the time I first sit on it, after which I fraternise with your bench regularly – eavesdrop on pigeons, watch the kites, reverie of kissing.

Name a species of kiss – this bench has seen them all, whether: an out-of-the-blue-leap-into-new-territories kiss; a soft-on-the-forehead-it's-going-to-be-okay kiss; a scrappy-tongue-lasher-spilling-out-the-sides kiss; the carnal-queen-bee-I-want-everything kiss; pashes, winches, shifts; a kiss for the first or the thousandth time; lips wet and bulging like mating slugs.

As I list kisses a storm bays in the sky and soon rain missiles down. I soak in it until my hair falls over my eyes like over-cooked spaghetti. I have seen it spiral unashamedly long to become a bulwark between me and the world. I let the hirsute beast foment in order to remind myself how much thinking is still to be done.

. . .

The memoir *A Grief Observed* by C. S. Lewis is posted under my studio door by a chum – decorating its inside cover a consoling pencil etching (brazen curlicues). The chum's name is Scotty and he's been a libertine, a mod, a new romantic, a football casual and several swoops of fashion in between.

More recently, back in Edina, Scotty packed in his job as a supplies manager of a chartered accountants to be a full-time writer. Not a single paid publication to his name, yet off he skittered to have a crack at the writerly profession. Gallus as fuck from the moment I met him in 2004 dancing alone in the kitchen of a trendy house party – dancing with his top off to Counting Crows as the living room hipsters discussed mescaline experiences and contenders for the Turner Prize. I stripped off and joined in.

The copy of *A Grief Observed* Scotty gave me is an old Faber classic, the colour of delicately minted toothpaste. Originally published under the name N. W. Clerk, the slim volume is a detailed recollection by C. S. Lewis (the author of, *inter alia*, *The Chronicles of Narnia*) of his experiences in grief and bereavement upon losing his wife. His conclusions (over the sixty-nine pages) are both trenchant and mordant.

A salient point C. S. Lewis makes is that 'passionate grief does not link us with the dead but cuts us off from them'.

He then crumples into passionate grief, crippling any such sureness. The conclusion I reach from his writings is that each experience with grief is capable of fully contradicting the last.

Many striking theories and statements dwell in C. S. Lewis's memoir. The first being the key to a healthy relationship – not idolising each other and knowing each other's rotten parts. The second being the way he described his love in grief, as if observed by the ghost of loss, reduced to its component measures of tinsel and froth.

Much of *A Grief Observed* was integrated into a film about C. S. Lewis (*Shadowlands*); I've yet to watch it. I look forward to uncovering more well-portrayed male grief in films. Films that depict the grieving man throwing himself into feckless cage fighting scenarios or bar brawls that can't be won are far too prevalent – punching fuck out of mirrors or crashing cars as a means of numbing pain. This says male grief is best served violent, carnaptious, suited to thrashing movements, born of storm. This says breaking down is only acceptable when accompanied by battles, exhaustion or grave injury. I gravely disagree.

C. S. Lewis's observations of grief corkscrew, plié and unspool with steady inconsistencies – a tightrope walk of rational contradictions and hapless despair. I nod along with vehemence, at times cheeping 'yes' and 'me too' and 'that's it' and other concurring commentaries. Of course, it dawned upon me, this brilliantly written and very godly examination of loss is again centred on the absence of a spouse – labelled 'front line' bereavement.

In any battle analogy, the front line is the most dangerous place to be. It's the leading position. But what's behind the front line? A second line? Reserve trenches? Majors discussing tactics from a safe distance with runners to bridge the gap between them and the action? My military knowledge wanes beyond this tart analogy, but it does get me thinking about the hierarchies in grief. The worry that arises out of perceptions of precedent and order, the decorum implicit in the manner in which we grieve.

Most people lose a grandparent before anyone closer – the family tree's furthest branches break off. That's the nuclear formula, right? It feels unusual to say we're lucky if it happens this way, but we are. Though most likely we'll find it hard to feel lucky and there's no guarantees this will mollify the loss or temper the grief in any way. It's always worth bearing in mind that alongside any loss is a web of further losses – all the ripples beyond the immediate; it's never easy to gauge death's impact. The loss of one precious human can cause every member of that family to have to recalibrate who they are within the nexus and how they relate to each other now. Some people are pivotal to the way we interact with others.

When my strength and reason are at their apotheosis, I feel part of all places and factions, entitled to my grief, a disciple to the incantations of Elton John singing 'The Circle of Life' in *The Lion King*. I simply concentrate on making you proud. When of a more frangible temperament, every outburst seems greedy and comes with a guilty post-match debrief. Was I entitled to buckle when those with closer links to you maintained a strong demeanour? Should I have been distributing succour rather than crumbing down to bird feed? Of the currency in me, I do not want to share too much nor too little – where's the balance?

This is the psychological heave of grief, the mind jousting with itself. But wounds' needs cauterised, and there's a collectivism to be found in healing. If trees can heal each other indiscriminately surely human bodies can too. Wise mother trees dole out subsistence to the saplings, elders embolden the young, old friends move their branches out the way of the sun to let the light in, woody whispers pass in wind. This accumulation of friendly action is what the German forester and author Peter Wohlleben calls the 'Wood Wide Web'.

We can learn from trees, from their friendly actions and the habits of those that respect them. Our lives are just a flash in the pan compared to the living of a bristlecone pine or sacred fig – all the night and day we see, all the stars we serenade, nary a note in their humongous opera. On this earth there is a tree nearly five thousand years old. Gandalf's staff, tree. Hermione's broomstick, tree. Young Zelda's shield, tree. That said, trees can't toss a rope swing over us.

. . .

In the grand scheme of things (certainly compared to a giant redwood) our friendship was a pup, lithe and giddy with voice still breaking. It existed, oh god yes, but where does that leave me now you're gone?

People's expectations of our grief can become an acute source of anxiety – when is too soon for a public engagement;

can I share my good news; just how candidly can pain be written down then read aloud; should I cancel my birthday party; does this elegy distort someone else's version of the truth; what about a wedding; just how seriously are you taking this; when is it okay to start laughing again; can I post this sexy-looking selfie?

The imposing nature of grief hierarchies – where we sit within the mourning group; our presupposed rank amongst the front-line grievers – is merely evidence of us reaching for reassurance at a time when everything appears to be crumbling. It's the search for straight-talking truths when faced with a cacophony of disparate advice, alongside dealing with our own anxious reticence. In certain cultures, there is a firmly established grieving period, an allocated number of days of relief within a predetermined timeframe; a costume that should be worn. The idea of such an instructive custom seems momentarily enviable.

How we mourn our friends might ultimately stem from how we interacted while they were here. But seeing as there's no contract for friendship – the way there is for marriage or employment – it's no wonder we're left so totally discombobulated when things go awry.

But what if such a contract did in fact exist?

Somewhere inside our minds we already have our own tenets and principles for friendship. We expect loyalty and kindness from the friends we love – at least equal to the level we're prepared to give.

From the outset, such a contract would require fidelity to the notion that friendship is closely linked to forgiveness. We are forever making sacrifices and altering our expectations to hold on to our friends. Such protean thinking would require new clauses constantly – a contract that could grow with grace: each clause cut from an instance of us at our best and worst selves.

An example of this? I call to the stand my mucker The Cous.

Moving out of my first London flat on Hibernia Street (where I lived with Ted and Rodriguez took transitory refuge) and being sent on secondment to the Wellcome Trust triggered an auspicious change of pace and circumstance. I lucked out with a property above some dear friends in Kentish Town, on a leafy street, with a balcony and a roof garden. Season into that Kentish Town being connected by an overground train to Euston, eliminating the need for any rush-hour tube travel. A big-city / London-specific type of bliss, but one that oiled the springs in the summer and took the ice off my engine in the winter.

The Cous offered to power down from Leith and help move me in to this new abode. A visit which coincided with meeting my new landlord – Greek Tony.

Tony had left the keys with the friends below, so we were already in, but he wanted to stop by and give me the once-over. Tony owned the entire townhouse cut up into four separate apartments, with a shabby little office on the Holloway Road where we had to drop off rent (cash or cheque). I think he aspired to be a wily wheeler-dealer type but was too lazy and disorganised. In his tatty clothes, he appeared the type of man who was constantly itchy.

As a flat-warming present The Cous had decided to purchase

some reading material for me – the magazine variety. Deeming it such an interesting spread he cut the publication into individual pages and tacked or taped them over the walls of the house. The most fruitfully decorated area was the upstairs living room, which was generously garlanded by ten or so pages. The very spot where landlord Tony was sitting when I arrived home from work.

The Cous was out on the balcony in denim shorts and a Rab C. Nesbitt-style vest. One leg lunged up on the railings, sucking the life out of a deck of cigarettes and demolishing a six-pack of Stella, whilst regaling Tony with stories about his fraught love life and quarrelsome faither. I feel inclined to note The Cous is unavoidably handsome.

The dissected periodical in question was a pornographic magazine – not a *Playboy*, no, a cheaper Eurotrash equivalent. Galleried around Tony, sinking into the couch like a marshmallow into hot chocolate, was everything from loaded cum shots to squirty cream explosions, and what appeared to be a foursome splayed over a snooker table. The Cous beamed bright, all seventh heaven for his own curation.

Neither Tony nor I acknowledged the fleshy artworks as he sipped tea and took me through the formalities of the new tenancy. Weirdly, the awkwardness swiftly subsided as I jotted signatures over the two-page lease – incredulous at the paucity of detail in the document compared to those I'd been drafting at work.

Tony moseyed off content with a brief glance in The Cous's direction. The Cous would later profess they'd bonded.

Had Tony been a more ambitious landlord I posit I might have been on thin ice from henceforth and subject to regular inspections. I would learn inspections were something Tony would dutifully arrange but rarely carry out – perhaps there was caution enough in their scheduling.

If a contract for friendship had existed between The Cous and me, then a mélange of potential breaches occurred on this day.

The Cous had been requested to make himself scarce when Tony arrived. Recommended to head to the friendly neighbour's house for a libation or canter into Camden to scout the streets for drinking companions. Cavalier, he did neither.

The Cous had been requested not to smoke in the flat. I had agreed with Tony this would be a non-smoking flat. I intended to break this rule but not so blatantly, nor so soon. I can't recall but I surmise the cigarette butts were flicked with moxie off the balcony into the gardens beyond, Tony in plain sight, as I winced. I later learned the cigarettes and cans were still to be paid for and left as a tab in my name at the local newsagent.

The Cous had not strictly been prohibited from purchasing a pornographic magazine, separating the pages and erecting them all over the property, but I like to think I'd instilled in him the impression this was not something I'd vote in favour of. More so if this ceremony was to occur during a landlord's property induction.

All in all, a breach-peppered incident within the expectations of our mooted contract for friendship.

But The Cous is a mate; he can be an incorrigible cunt but I knew the risks of accepting his offer of help. I am inured to his gnarly bits and rapscallion ways. Plus, the loyalty and support he's given me over the years more than balance out these aberrations of judgement. He's a carnival of fun, brutish whilst tender. He's hefting a battered heart around, has suffered let-downs and family complexities. The Cous when chipper to me groggy is like the smell of warm bread waking up a hungry sleeper.

This two-day visit turned into two weeks; in the end I had to courier him back to Edinburgh personally. But the overnight Megabus home was eventful and I've got mileage out these stories. And to be fair, he did offer Tony a can and a fag, though my landlord had to make his own tea – not The Cous's forte back then. Besides, it's not as if it was Tony's birthday.

It would be remiss of me not to make a footnote to this story or, more accurately, I'll risk a clobbering. The Cous now lives on the Isle of Skye, where he works various seasonal jobs, often in the grounds of ancient castles, basking in campestral vastness. To make this a still more idyllic picture, he's bought a plot of land and is piece by piece building a croft with the support of his family.

He no longer hammers the bevvy, has turned his hand to claymation, and is considered in his actions. He is the friend I recognised he would be and sacrificed for, looking past all manner of breaches.

I fucking love The Cous.

With The Cous as our stanchion, I advocate that contracts for friendship would be an invaluable addition to the UK legal system. Their cluster of clauses serving as evidence of the storms people weather and the obstacles they overcome in honour of connection. What a boon it would be to have a contract narrated by what might be termed a moral compass – a life story charted through the mishaps and burdens we bear in order to keep our dear people dear. (Like most great things within the realms of contracts) valid in equity if not by the black letter law. I call upon Scotland to lead the way.

. . .

In Terese Marie Mailhot's book *Heart Berries* she notes that: 'Sometimes suicidality doesn't seem dark; it seems fair.' She also said that in her culture it is holy to fall apart. I think so too – you have a song about this that you once described as the reason we're such good friends.

Books, music and films are supreme aids for an ailing mind, especially when benevolently gifted. Photos, too, I covet when raw – an image to match each emotive state is becoming part of my day's vocabulary. On top of those I've amassed, I've been sent a miscellany of pictures I never knew existed. Scrolling through my ever-increasing collection has become an obsession. But is a phone full of treasured photos visited daily conducive to betterment, or am I feeding a seedy fix? I scroll through these images, study the expressions, hoover up insights into our lighter psyches.

Photo of us in the Cape Town Aquarium – note the shorts (2017). Photo of us eating oysters together for the first time in New York (2015). Photo of us wearing matching leopard-print robes in Joburg's Hallmark House hotel (2017). Photo of you on the Silver Sands of Morar rejecting the rope swing, kicking pebbles into the trim of the deep (2018). Photo of us, Kevin and Bill Ryder-Jones posing like a boy band outside the Waverley Bar after my first book launch (2013). Photo of us backstage at the final gig we did together at Glasgow Art School for Lake of Stars (2018). Photo of you with M'hudi in hand at Paradise Restaurant (2018). Photo of us the first night we met at Neu! Reekie! (2012). Photo of you and Hollie sitting across from me, eyeing up pudding – one last supper in Mallarn (2018). This final photo I have printed on a tea-towel and magic mug.

I resurrect the memories in my photos any time I feel a maudlin clutch (*el perro negro*) tightening around my chest. But it's no sure thing, a digital elixir one day is a gut puncher the next – it's all so stubbornly changeable.

What the photos say is that sometimes your happiness belonged to me, as it did with others: friends, family, lovers. And for small periods of time, each of us was responsible for it, custodians; breathing together like a pair of lungs – sharing haemoglobin, oxygenating.

What the photos don't say is that, in general, the happiness people need is bigger and more esoteric than we are able to ascertain – it's crucial to remember this. I must not inveigle myself or infantilise my importance. It is hard to admit there was no love I could have given you that would have prevented this tragedy. Hard to admit but probably true – just like the fact that you are six months gone.

. . .

I have a November tradition with Paris. I spent a month in Grez-sur-Loing on the Robert Louis Stevenson Fellowship in 2015. Grez, a historic commune just south of Paris, has been popular with artists and free-thinkers for hundreds of years. Here Robert Louis Stevenson (author of *Treasure Island* and *The Strange Case of Dr Jekyll and Mr Hyde*) wrote, bided, and met his wife-to-be. And here, on his Fellowship, I penned the poems that became our *Oyster*. Romantically roused (and let's face it who doesn't hanker after a dalliance with Paris), I vowed to journey back each November.

All these Paris trips were flavoured by Beaujolais Nouveau – a wine that launches young and coltish on the third Thursday of November to a bracing bacchanal; my favourite wine until, of course, M'hudi came along and stole the crown.

Like all good series, my Paris-in-November tradition has a pilot programme that starts even earlier. I caught you playing a gig here on your birthday in November 2013. They lit you in indigo blue and sunflower yellow; you wore a salmon shirt. Afterwards, we emptied cups and chatted: about how this hip venue (Point Éphémère) had more of a Berlin aesthetic – feeling super suave by saying so; about how you were looking forward to the tour coming to a close and what a galactic heave it had been.

When ruminating with Hollie where I wanted to be on your birthday (because these things need acting on) I instinctively vied for Paris.

I think you would cheer for us here, five years on, back in Point Éphémère celebrating the occasion. Engaging in a rollicking game of ping-pong; ordering nibbles and drowning them in sauce; poking our heads into the concert space and taking a bite out it; clinking to your triumph – keeping it zesty, as birthdays rightly should be.

I imagined you were with us and so the night felt spattered with your quiddity. There was a flick in the flame of a candle I couldn't take my eyes off.

. . .

I love Christmas. I have forever deemed Christmas trees the greatest harbingers of joy. Christmas is a catalyst for soppiness amongst friends, for seeing each other no matter the cost.

For the first time this year I do the Christmas tree trail in Glasgow's West End as well as Leith. Thousands of folks have theatrically decorated firs, spruces and plastic epigones at great expense, and yet even the most assiduously crafted ensembles are still a little vulgar. Some of the trees are practically invisible from the inside, serving more as seasonal lighthouses. They say: ahoy out there in the darkness / we're celebrating / we hope this finds that heart candle-wax warm / safe home. Yes it's fleeting, yes it's prescribed and commercialised, not for everyone; nonetheless this refulgence makes my bones glow. You did not feel the same but enjoyed my glee. It was a big talking point between us. You would not be surprised to see this partisan parcel of words bedecking the page. I'd take the friendly fire that followed.

A pre-eminent tree reminds me of one of my most canonised achievements – getting you to wear a Christmas shirt for our Cold Turkey show in December 2017. Sure you taunted the snow cottage-clad garment on stage and only slipped it on for our group finale, but what a fucking cameo.

. . .

Happy Christmas. Mine is a vegetarian dinner and a bottle of Champagne; a toast to you with my best jumper on.

. . .

Having spent the last couple of Hogmanay celebrations with you in Edinburgh, I choose to flee the country with some pals. We take a cheap apartment in Seville and count in the New Year amongst the hordes at the Plaza Nueva fiesta. The future's starry blur has piqued the interest of thousands of travellers. Each among us is choosing which worries to untether in order to make way for new promise. The tradition here is to arrive with friends and stuff a grape into the mouth with the chime of each bell as it bongs towards midnight. Twelve grapes resembling good fortune for the year ahead. A fun twist on this ritual is to squirrel all twelve into the mouth at once and kiss the cheeks of each in the posse before gobbling them back.

Juice oozing everywhere, New Year's clarion call rattles my brain. I have been becoming steadily more saccharine about dates and anniversaries, increasingly quixotic about their significance. Some days my skin is whipped to cream by a simple social media reminder.

The year changing is a big moment; it comes caped and crusading, thought to be hostile, then passes coolly. I realise Hogmanay was just the dress rehearsal, for never far from my mind is a bolder question: what will happen when a year lapses of you being gone?

I start the New Year not with a countdown but with a noise, which could simply be the hiss of streetlamps; then again it does sound like ticking.

. . .

With my Bréon I journey back to The Abbey Hotel. It's April, and I'm hoping the newly hatched spring plays a blinder. The room lottery allocates him the Willie Gunn suite and me a room called Garry – a felicitous start.

In the day we walk Scotland's southern fringes and take a visit to Smailholm Tower. In the evening we talk about dark forces gathering and the notion of towers within the armoury of life. You are eleven months gone and Bréon is checking in.

The next morning, he heads off early to Edina, leaving me at the breakfast buffet, where the song 'All by Myself' jangles out speakers at a tepid volume – the Celine Dion version. I am sitting alone in a large and nearly empty room, reading a death and mental health memoir, in a hotel I've come to only once before for reasons of saying farewell. Couldn't write it.

Initially I submit to the mawkishness, but then the funny side clatters into the stiff dining room and starts swinging from the faux chandelier. Out the window the forest unfurls like a giant caterpillar straightening its curl, a convoy of jazzy greens. In creeps the notion that perhaps I'm not so alone after all. Then a swan shrieks and settles it.

. . .

To get to Shetland, over land and sea, from Glasgow is a grand gest. Bill Drummond picks us (team Neu! Reekie!) up at George Square and we drive to Aberdeen in around three hours. At Aberdeen Ferry Terminal we board a huge vessel that will carry us overnight to Lerwick – we have bunks. The ferry crosses a tumultuous run of the North Sea, taking a total of thirteen hours. From Lerwick it's on to Unst – Shetland's most northerly isle.

On Unst, we assist Bill in presenting his film at Baltasound Hall. It's well attended and fills the rooms with intrigue. I adore Bill's unending relish; he's done more with his one life than most do with ten – cultivating ideas and enkindling action like there's no tomorrow. And just as well, for some there's not.

After the show we stay in an old RAF facility that feels incongruous to the evening's allure, but it does have a lovely conservatory from which to watch the sky's lucent sparkle.

The following morning an attendee of the film screening, a man called Tony, invites our group to pay him a visit. We take him up on the offer because Tony lives in Muckle Flugga Shore Station – the northmost inhabited house on the British Isles. Prior to Tony's stewardship, it would have been the home of the keeper of Muckle Flugga Lighthouse.

Tony implores our touring party to share his solitude and stare off into the abysm. I watch the sun baste the landscape, baking the colours verdurous. Watch the water pulse and thrash, pretending I too lived as a lighthouse. The fact that Muckle

Flugga Lighthouse once had a young Robert Louis Stevenson in its clutches makes the spot all the more beguiling. RLS journeyed here to learn the family trade of lighthouse engineering, told to put the pithy career of writing behind him. The stint, in fact, did the opposite – raised his gusto like a storm.* The local populace influenced the cast of *Treasure Island* and, some say, its infamous map is modelled on Unst's sashay.

Lighthouses are another thing that will always remind me of you. Why? You drew them well. That moment in the light gallery of the tiny lighthouse we crammed into at the fountainhead of the road trip. Julia Darling's poem that starts: 'I would like us to live like two lighthouses / at the mouth of a river, each with her own lamp. / We could see each other across the water / which would be dangerous, and uncrossable.'

The water and waves that carried you will have moved far by now and some of your salt may have found its way here. I hope so because then you'd hear the choir of raucous seabirds that we are obviously disturbing. The showy chieftains, who pirouette the sky and pilot snarling winds, dive bomb in our vicinity to mark their turf. I hope so because it's beautiful here and you should have known that instead of being eleven-and-a-half months gone.

I fly back from Shetland on a fun-sized toy of a Logan Airplane, twelve seats (half taken), powered by propellers not

---

* That said, RLS did compromise and study a law degree as a safety harness against the perils of pursuing a literary career, but who could blame him for that!

much bigger than adult arms. Gazing down on where humans build their lives, unable to move any of the pieces of my own, I think: what a lot of people trying to get this right.

. . .

Portobello's pinch of coastline along the Firth of Forth, peering off to Fife, carries something different now, no two looks into this sea will ever be the same since you left.

I head off, like the cell door has just been opened, on a nostalgic rove along Portobello promenade. Compared to twenty years ago, its ocean is cleaner and better swam in, the Turkish baths have been restored, and the French bulldog population is soaring. The towering high school of my youth razed, replaced by a slick new building, with much change afoot on the high street. It may soon merit the *Guardian*'s 'Rio-like' write-up.

I'm reminded of a day back in 2014 when a sperm whale washed up on the Joppa end of Porty beach – rumour had it, nicked in the neck by a ship's propeller and bled out. The friends I was with at the time, who dated back to schooldays, insisted we venture down to join the gawking crowds. Though uneasy, their alacrity trumped my reluctance and off we shot before I could think of a better reason not to. No confusing where to head: a passel of lively spectators marked the spot like a fête. Beyond the corral of people, a motionless leviathan of marbled grey, collapsed on the shallows and opened up. This was the first whale I'd seen in the flesh, blood, like last light, weeping out of it. The throng edged closer, as both experts and gulls investigated its meat. This was *Moby-Dick* crossed with Orwell's 'Shooting an Elephant'. The whale, thirty tons of death, a lugubrious reminder even giants die. My phone pinged as my friend Danny tried to check us in at 'the carcass' on Facebook.

I exit the promenade and take to Portobello High Street, where I stumble upon an evocative site – Mike's Tackle Shop, not just closed but sold. I'm happy to see it changing hands and peer through the window fully expecting to be sucked into a time warp.

Mike's Tackle Shop was a popular lunchtime and after-school rendezvous for all the fishing aficionados in my year. I'd regularly be dragged there by boy friends who could spend hours trawling the shelves, pawing at hooks and mallets and gaping at the framed pictures of champion fishermen. I did like the natural elements of fishing trips and its bonding opportunities, but the gathering of equipment and the showboating of prize catches was lost on me. As was the aggrandising of the supposed manliness of the sport: the hunting element, the showing-off of scars, the war-like tactics in building up an arsenal.

For an epoch (in the late nineties and early noughties), these trips to the tackle shop became frequent pilgrimages. Alongside the nuisance of lost hours was that of feigning an interest in the stories of the elder huntsmen who lingered there – slow-moving tales of fish clobberings told with little panache. Nothing noxious, just a drawn-out affair of stifled emotionality.

The visits to the tackle shop were rigmarole, burble that held me back from getting out into landscape. Yet this mulling about in the shop was something boys did, a banal rite of passage, and

I wanted to fit in and be included in the (relatively few) resulting outings. So there I was, as ensnared by this pesky ritual as the muckle fish in the photos that adorned the walls.

Staring into the shop window, I consider how the notion of 'Gone Fishing' serves as a trope for males flocking off with other males to steep in silence and address difficult 'matters'. Fathers off fishing with sons, absolutely, but friends with friends foremost. It offers a safe haven to expose tenderness that wouldn't (to some shouldn't) come out under other circumstances. In this way, fishing trips are synonymous with male bonding – it's nature, isolation and solitude made palatable by the banner of sport. Naturally, this was not the way for me, who was clumsily spilling out sentiment here, there and everywhere – in all the wrong places. I found these designated safe spaces to explore male sensitivity too staid, slow and diluted, too few and far between.

It didn't feel like the 'done thing' growing up in Scotland in the nineties and noughties but I couldn't do it any other way. I would tell my friends I loved them constantly, with humility, be soppy, undeterred by the rowel and rankle of others' or my own trepidations. My friends and I, we hugged, we cried, we talked about our fears and vulnerabilities – we were naked together. It's something that grew with time and now I'm way past the point of noticing these behaviours may not fit politely into the algebra of most male relationships. With the friends I've lost, I regret having not done this more.

The 'Gone Fishing' trope is a pattern of behaviour now alien to me, the antithesis of the type of relationship I had with you. It took years of candour, bravery and heartache to break the constraints of my own thinking about male friendship and unlock a new mode of loving that empowers me still. Years, but worth every fumble and thrust. No apologia for the slushiness; why be pious to grief but not to love?

I learn the site of Mike's Tackle Shop will in fact (coincidentally or perhaps cosmically) soon become Portobello Bookshop. A new indie, collective-run, word emporium, indicative of the changing tune of the area. On discovering these plans, I hear the younger me lament Portobello Bookshop not being around when I was squandering my lunchtimes looking at hooks. More than this, my younger self extols new opportunities for the next generation of Porty dwellers. For a first bookshop, in an area that's long been without one, absolutely widens the scope for sentient relationships – through reading groups, literary events, author visits and encounters with curious humans. At a push, it has an occult magnetism. Where mallets once hung, poetry stacks the shelves.

. . .

Friendship is a constitution, a formation; 'friend' comes from the same root as 'freedom'.

The etymology of 'friend' is my ally. *Frēond* in Old English stems from, among other wordy scions, the Proto-Germanic *frijōjands*. The root 'fr' meaning 'to love', being attached to another by feelings. Into Old English the word trots, becoming synonymous with relationships of strong feelings, feelings not necessarily familial or sexual, but just as worthy.

There's a wee period later in Old English where 'friend' can also mean its antonym 'enemy'. And then some Middle English brouhaha where it links into trusted money lending, yet 'friend' emerges triumphant and settles into a nest of positive connotations of closeness and fondness. 'Friend' is joined by such cute complications as 'girlfriend' and 'boyfriend', and then carnally charged euphemisms of the 'lady friend' genus. 'Boy friend' is yet to truly find its place – on the world's leading word processor it will trigger a grammatical error.

. . .

In Edinburgh's Waverley Station, I bump into a friend. He clasps my hand and begs me be in touch more often. He tells me that he'll be thinking of me, that he knows it's going to hurt hellfire. He knows you are fifty-one weeks gone and soon to be anniversaried. The magnitude of his words balloons because of this skin-to-skin connection. Saying this while holding my hand gestures that he's not going anywhere. These aren't words spoken as we splinter off into the next stage of the day; they're here and now and come with a heartbeat. He is testament to the undiminishable power in holding hands.

Boys holding hands, men holding hands, boys becoming men holding hands throughout. This is a conventional expression of friendship in many countries. One photographer capturing men holding hands in India enquired as to why they were doing so. The muses seemed baffled by the question and chanted back proudly, 'Because we are best friends.'

The sign language for friends is achieved by hooking your

two index fingers in C shapes – linking them together and then swapping them around, a back-and-forth finger hug. Another, more British, method is clasping your secondary hand with your primary hand in front of your body and moving them carefully up and down. Enough said.

Sometimes with close male friends I take their hand in a notable moment and see how long they hold for. Some snap back as if singed, some tactically recoil, others act out a playful parody of a happy couple, exaggerated yet fugacious. A few just go with it, blithesome, seeing the benefit, and keep the confab churning.

My friend here in Waverley Station, he's of the final, favourite category. Ready to part, we hug heavy. In the carpeting sun, I watch our shadows blob together, becoming a single vessel, a sketch of Vishnu with wilder hair. Although our shadow bodies part, something within us will stay together more indelibly.

. . .

Tonight I open for the band Idlewild at Glasgow's iconic Barrowlands venue. Had you been here, it is likely we would have done this together, as we'd done so in the past.

Remember? It's when that friendly heckler demanded you remove your socks and hilarity ensued as you attempted to parse the purpose behind this perplexing request. 'Take your socks off' is a unique crotchet of a heckle. Especially if howled over the top of a huge crowd during the quiet of a minor key change. You were quite right to attempt to get to the bottom of it – did they mean socks off but shoes still on? Or was it a slip of tongue and what they actually meant was shoes off but socks on?

Devoid of an answer to this pressing question, but equipped with my friend Eugene for company, I open for Idlewild without you on Saturday, 4 May 2019. A significant date, being a year on from us together in Croon, the first night of a road trip from which you never return.

In my head I have climbed through a time portal and emerged twelve months back at Croon harbour, clueless as to what would soon unfold. While in reality, I am on stage at the Barrowlands, tumbling out poems to revellers, scanning another disco ball for your face. I mention your name (once out loud and a hundred times more behind my eyelashes) and the crowd erupt in applause. I wear a T-shirt with your illustration sunned across my chest and take my shoes off (evincing the socks / a pair you gave me) so as they might remember us together.

As I finish the set, I breathe in deeply in the hope that one of your atoms remained here and will pull itself inside me.

Towards night's close Idlewild cover one of your songs. People cheer for your story still stretching out. The applause – all kinetic energy – bests the bruising.

. . .

Over morning coffee, I watch the sun make up its mind how bold a role to play in the day. I can relate. A six-hour drive to Ullapool from Edinburgh awaits.

Earlier in the year, Ullapool Book Festival invited me back to read and say some things about the show we never did together in May 2018. I accepted and looped in Hollie and (singer friend) Withered Hand, because the event will fall on 10 May (the day you were found) and such an excursion, to the emotional verge, should not be taken alone.

Although the border is blurred, and there is a penumbra over time that does not afford an utter precision, it is on *this* day, 9 May 2019, that I think of you as one year gone.

The ache in my bones from missing you is a year old – the twelve months have been an austere education. I'm more attuned to the pathos of Russian literature and the confessional poetry of Anne Sexton and Sylvia Plath than I hoped to be. Though painful, the arrival of this day comes with a countenance; it is not without mercy.

In these peewee maxims (this *ars poetica* on missing) I settle some things.

Making moments a celebration of your life rather than a lament of your death used to sound like a starry-eyed hippie mantra – better a slogan slapped onto a mug than a tool for prosaic living. Miraculously, over the year, it's become much more achievable than I deemed possible. My first instinct *is* now to grasp at reason to celebrate. There will be weepy bits that come part and parcel of each occasion, but they're simply side effects of a bigger purpose.

Healing is not disloyal to any memory. I frequently forget the horror and don't rebuke myself for seeking escapisms.

In the months after you left, I was cankerous about misplacing any detail; a single lost frame from the spool of life arrived like a vision of doom. I am easier now if I need to recreate a memory from a thing part-formed. There is beauty in the not knowing – our life, a mystery even to ourselves.

Of memories: in the process of remembering you I have uprooted instances where I errantly fused two separate memories together, tinkering with the plot of the past. Splitting the molecules apart reveals my mind's auditor already knew more than I suspected. Memories get more gnostic the longer we spend in them; they are distance travelled within the body. *

When I find myself drawn to the frenzy, I've learnt to pull back, to think slower and sleep longer – processes taken as automatic I've been mindful of so as to help them help me.

When you left I carried you into every moment, hijacked the present's freshness over and over. Now you come and go as you please, no need to keep me posted.

Some things remain beyond explanation.

American poet Charles Wright said: 'Grief is a floating barge-boat, who knows where it's going to moor?' Hollywood sweetheart Keanu Reeves said: 'grief changes shape but never ends'. I think in reference to the loss of his friend River Phoenix, but then it may have been a wider quote because that man has seen a lot of loss (yet remains a beacon).

---

* The advances neuroscience is making in activating and manipulating memories is mind-boggling, but a conversation beyond this footnote. Suffice to say, keep an eye out for new neural machinery that might turn our mind into a time-travelling device. How important then to do our own manual due diligence before movies such as *Eternal Sunshine of a Spotless Mind*, *Total Recall* and *Inception* become reality.

What the year has proven, in the main part, is that tens of thousands of people have been revived by your words, thousands of them want to be bolder for having heard you.

I and many others think of you daily as an impetus to make courageous and difficult choices, to overcome fear and anxiety. We burrow you deep into our psyches, will talk to you all our lives, integrating your bravery into our existence. Wounds will heal and gallant and righteous things will happen because of you, because of what you wrote and sang and the strength in it. Few humans will pull together this many kindred spirits for a common and collective good. I am so proud to have known you.

It's vitally important to keep talking about those we miss, the wonder they unleashed, the immense talent they possessed and the joy they furnished upon our faces. Keep paddling in their river-ing tales. We all miss people to levels it's hard to comprehend; we are lost and confused yet that is the very thing that bands us together.

People are gone and now we have to work out how to turn the love they gave us into something we won't forget: music, poetry, laughter. Like our South African dream of a taxi driver, Clarence Prince, would say (as if a catchphrase): 'It was my pleasure travelling with such precious cargo.' Anywhere you would have gone, I'd have gone there too, and in many ways am still going.

The drive to Ullapool offers moments of elation as well as ripe reflection. We drive over the Forth Road Bridge and play your music loud. We stop at House of Bruar. We arrive.

. . .

On the morning of the show, we snake up Ullapool Hill, walk the wilderness, applaud its bravado.

In the coconut pant of the wind-rattled gorse, which studs the journey up then down, is an olfactory reminder of looking for you. The same familiar fragrance loaded into the Ullapool air perfumed Fife's coastal pathways on our painstaking search. But up here, on this day – in this maze of gloss, gaps and silence – we know that you've left; it is so sad, but there is peacefulness in the knowledge that cushions us.

At the show, Withered Hand goes on last and describes you as a Wounded Healer, having spent serious time thinking on the matter. Sapiently, he declares this from the stage in a hot propelling voice. He flushes the words out, stressing what a great big wow it had been to sail alongside you; how lucky we were to have hatched such dreams. It connects as if he spoke from scripture. Long live the love you gave us; it sung louder than any stereo could.

As the show wraps up – to give way to a ceilidh we vehemently participate in – I rake over these thoughts, ensorcelled by the music and new moniker, wishing you had heard it.

. . .

I have just viewed the final episode of *Game of Thrones* on my own in Glasgow. It's silly but it felt like a big hurdle. I expected to see your name skittle into the credits and thought if you were going to turn up this might have been the time. I wept all spider leg trembles then hear you say, 'Winter is coming, you dick,' as a summer night cosied in. I flip back to the start, begin again my watch.

. . .

I take a late May amble through Edinburgh's Holyrood Park as the morning sun and new-sprung wind tussle with ducks for bread they shouldn't be fed. Geese honk at precious canines with tinkling collars. I am on my way to Summerhall to host a workshop searching for a spoken-word star. I will tell them only what I know as gospel: that reading lots of poetry is more likely to make you a better poet than anything else.

I take the long way around – yes, a sharp left at the gorse bush that blimps bolshie above the wildflowers, then onto the walkway below St Anthony's Chapel. You do know it; below the vertiginous path young frogs fling themselves up escaping greedy beaks – some make it; others turn to stone in the scorched heat and are there until winter when the frost swallows them whole. Poor dead frogs, so new to life the daisies live to be their elders.

So here I am, as you are everywhere, walking an aberrant path. The sun rampages the hillside, slicing it to strips. It is slung over the greenery like day-after remnants of a party that got out of hand. On my way, I funnel past a group of kids being marched around the park. It is European elections day, so voting is on and schools are off. The senior figure leading them is enthusiastic in a teacherly way. The whole parade reeks of that summer camp extracurricular pep that no-one's really fussed for.

The bulk of the boys come walking as one, gangling together, an unkempt foliage of trendy hats, hoodies, swish pumps and ubiquitous haircuts. Their cocky ringleader hangs like an injured soldier off the shoulders of his disciples, one on either side. They pass with the rising and falling in volume of a television drama, a sudden peak in sound as if a cat sat on the remote.

Behind them, one kid, solo, trundling along, twenty paces retracted from the swollen shadow of the pack. He's wearing ill-fitting blue denim jeans and a spongey woollen jumper. I think he looks sharp, the business. His hickory brown eyes trail the floor, weed-picking, mind in a tizzy or at least not where it should be. When we pass, he looks up, bangs right into my gaze. It shakes me. What a lot of noise about silence.

The boy seems on the edge of a frightened scream that could split rock. At the same time, it's as if he's readying himself to disappear into the ground through a gash in the earth he, with bare hands, will prise open. I prepare myself to witness the boy engulfed by soil, a landslide of him and insects tobogganing to the planet's core. I take a finger sting from a nettle to focus my mind and enliven the moment.

Now I could have misread the situation, but to me this wee soul had been ostracised, his fluffy jumper as out of tune with the hot weather as he is with the music of the clique. As I say, there's the possibility he cut back through choice, tired of their adulation; there is the possibility he was exhausted by their drab conversation and sought refuge in the company of this volcanic giant of a hillside. All possible, but I think not. And if I am wrong, then these wishes are instead for the person I imagined him to be (part me, part you, part a thousand others) and the situation I have cooked up around him.

I wish for him your music. I wish for him candid conversations about emotion. I dream for him cherished friendships and within those friendships the reassurance that things will be better than in these painful moments. I yearn for him to know that there is wonder out there so gargantuan it will rival the coruscation of a star-spangled sky on the clearest night imaginable.

I think about talking to the boy; about slipping him a tenner; about complimenting his knitwear; about a second lap around the loch to nudge the gang leader in amongst the ducks; about being in his body and feeling his thoughts for long enough to work something out on his behalf. But in the end I head to my studio and write this story, write about you, praise the detail that I do not miss now that I would have certainly missed before. You have taught me so much and I'll forever be working on it.

Notes

2 *Write hard and clear* Attributed to Ernest Hemingway, this quote has been shared on innumerable inspirational quote databases, Pinterest boards and creative writing forums – I even found embroidered tank tops available bearing this totem statement (swiftly purchased). However, I cannot uncover where this word jumble was originally authored, so will instead refer to the Yukon Writers' Society who ran a workshop of the same name. https://www.yukonwriterssociety.com/workshops/aug12

25 *I feel things twice as much as you do* Although initially attributed to Counting Crows, further research leads me to believe I have misremembered and discombobulated these lyrics. I postulate these were my own gooey sentiments falsely credited to the aforementioned pithy music makers in my search for emotional validation. With apologies to the band. As it turns out, this quote is from the song 'Motorcycle Parts' by undercelebrated Glasgow band The Supernaturals – themselves sublime conjurers of an adroit emotive lyric. This finding is attributed exclusively to the proofreader – despite their 1998 album *A Tune A Day* being one of my most poured-over possessions around that period. An album I procured as part payment on a loan made to my sister.

146 *Aye money has ruined it* Irvine Welsh, *Dead Men's Trousers*, Penguin, 2018, pp. 21–22.

148 *You were a bird before we met* Katherine Kilalea, *One Eyed'd Leigh*, Carcanet, 2009, p. 7.

148 *Missing you is not agonising* Michael Pedersen, *Oyster*, Polygon Books, 2017, p. 55.

159 *Seems silly, doesn't it? A wedding.* From *Harry Potter and the Deathly Hallows – Part 1* (feature film script), Warner Brothers Pictures, 2010, based on J. K. Rowling's 2007 novel of the same name.

164 *he became his admirers* W. H. Auden, 'In Memory of W. B. Yeats' https://poets.org/poem/memory-w-b-yeats

188 *passionate grief does not link us* C. S. Lewis, *A Grief Observed*, Faber & Faber, 1966, p. 47.

197 *sometimes suicidality* Terese Marie Mailhot, *Heart Berries*, Bloomsbury, 2019, p. 39.

204 *I would like us to live like two lighthouses* This quote from the poem 'Two Lighthouses', copyright Julia Darling, is from *Indelible, Miraculous* the collected poems of Julia Darling published by Arc 2015 and printed with permission of the Estate of Julia Darling. http://juliadarling.co.uk/works/collaborations/painting/

213 *Grief is a floating barge-boat* Charles Wright, 'Toadstools', published in the *New Yorker* online on 3 May 2010: https://www.newyorker.com/magazine/2010/05/10/toadstools

Acknowledgements and Thanks

To my editor Alexa, whose sapience, panache, style and talent for storytelling helped shaped this book in every one of its umpteen incarnations and who has ameliorated my writing and the life beyond it. Thank you, profusely, for everything.

A gratitude extended to all the fantabulous team at Faber & Faber – for lending me your passion and prowess – in particular: Mo, Rachael, Kate, Hannah, Lizzie.

To my incredible agent, Becky, for the indefatigable support, belief and zest from day one. This literary family we've sculpted is the stuff of dream dust.

To Jon, whose design wizardry dresses this book, and whose accompanying friendship has been a wonderful gift. Thanks also to Nathaniel Russell for granting us use of his stunning illustration.

To Hollie, in some respects, neither I nor this would be here without you. You are gorgeous, clever, kind and inexorably inspiring. My heart.

To my Ma and Da, for the obvious gift of life and the myriad lessons taught, with deep love, in-between. My sister, for eventually stopping resenting my existence and since becoming a cherished ally. My wee granny, Jessie, for your pure joyousness – it buoys us all so much.

To my early readers and blurbers who whizzed through these words and produced such scrumptious notes of espousal.

To the stupendous bookshops that have supported this hatchling, and thousands of tomes beyond – a most notable mention for The Portobello Bookshop, Lighthouse Books and Shakespeare & Company.

To Oysters, and those who offered me places of sanctum during the murky bits – in particular Bill and The Curfew Tower, and Bréon with Cascaroni.

To those friends who appear in this book under their own name, by alias or nickname, by reference, rite or strict omission. Thank you for the stories, for letting me be part of yours, for bolstering and emboldening mine own. Long live this luminous love.

To the friends who appear in my life, outside of this book, under their own name, by alias or nickname, by reference, rite or strict omission. Long live our lucent love.

A supplementary non-exhaustive roll call:

Adam Andrew Angus Bill Billy Charlotte Chris Clee Craig Daljit Damian Dan Daniel Danny Davie Davy Dominic Elizabeth Emun Esa Euan Eugene Ewen Francis Garry Gavin Gemma Gerry Gianni Helen Hera Iain Irvine Jackie Jake James Jamie Janette Jeff Jennifer Jenny John Jonathan Jonny Juliette Kat Kathryn Kayus Kenny Kev Kevin Lee Liz Lobo Marjorie Mark Mathew Michael Naveed Ocean Omar Owen Rachel Rhys Rob Robbie Roland Ross Sandro Sarah Scotty

Sean Shirley Simon Stacey Stephen Stevie Ted Terri The Cous Tom Val W1 Ziggy Zippy and MANY more.

To Scott – my small, yet humble, tribute to your everlasting beauty. Long may it soar, smooch over us and scintillate.